MW00636051

Hands-on DevOps with Linux

Build and Deploy DevOps Pipelines Using Linux Commands, Terraform, Docker, Vagrant, and Kubernetes

Alisson Machado de Menezes

www.bpbonline.com

FIRST EDITION 2021

Copyright © BPB Publications, India

ISBN: 978-93-89423-488

All Rights Reserved. No part of this publication may be reproduced, distributed or transmitted in any form or by any means or stored in a database or retrieval system, without the prior written permission of the publisher with the exception to the program listings which may be entered, stored and executed in a computer system, but they can not be reproduced by the means of publication, photocopy, recording, or by any electronic and mechanical means.

LIMITS OF LIABILITY AND DISCLAIMER OF WARRANTY

The information contained in this book is true to correct and the best of author's and publisher's knowledge. The author has made every effort to ensure the accuracy of these publications, but publisher cannot be held responsible for any loss or damage arising from any information in this book.

All trademarks referred to in the book are acknowledged as properties of their respective owners but BPB Publications cannot guarantee the accuracy of this information.

Distributors:

BPB PUBLICATIONS
20, Ansari Road, Darya Ganj
New Delhi-110002
Ph: 23254990/23254991

DECCAN AGENCIES
4-3-329, Bank Street,
Hyderabad-500195
Ph: 24756967/24756400

MICRO MEDIA
Shop No. 5, Mahendra Chambers,
150 DN Rd. Next to Capital Cinema,
V.T. (C.S.T.) Station, MUMBAI-400 001
Ph: 22078296/22078297

BPB BOOK CENTRE
376 Old Lajpat Rai Market,
Delhi-110006
Ph: 23861747

To View Complete
BPB Publications Catalogue
Scan the QR Code:

Published by Manish Jain for BPB Publications, 20 Ansari Road, Darya Ganj, New Delhi-110002 and Printed by him at Repro India Ltd, Mumbai

www.bpbonline.com

Dedicated to

My Family and Friends

About the Author

Alisson Machado de Menezes is an experienced Big Data DevOps Engineer, who for the past ten years has been working in different positions, such as Developer, Operations Analyst, Support Analyst, DevOps Engineer, IT Manager, Technical leader and now diving into Big Data. Has many lectures in Brazil in events like Python Brasil, The Developers Conference, Feira Internacional de Software Livre and for some companies in private. Also gave classes regarding Python Programming, Agile Infrastructure, MongoDB, Openshift, Kubernetes, DevOps and DevSecOps. Has the certifications Linux System Administrator (LPIC-1), Linux Engineer (LPIC-2), Suse Certified Linux Administrator (SUSE CLA), LPIC – OT DevOps Tools Engineer, Exin – DevOps Professional and Studied English in Canada.

In 2019, Alisson moved to Germany starting a new challenge in Europe on the Automotive Marketing to help of Empower mobility for tomorrow, where we are trying to be the pioneers on Electrical Cars.

Outside work, Alisson tries to maintain a blog where he shares some experience on the project which he has been working and when there is time travelling, hiking and try different types of beer.

About the Reviewer

Leonardo Mendes is currently working as a Software Reliability Engineer and core member of the technology innovation team at Cogna. He focuses on FOSS (Free and Open Source Software) projects. He is passionate about training and worked in projects of Education, coordinating the training team in the delivery of Linux, DevOps, Cloud and Big Data training, also participate in the implementation projects, and teaching the courses about Linux, DevOps, Cloud.

He is graduated from Computer Networking and has MBA at Cloud Computing.

Acknowledgement

There are a few people I want to thank for the continued and ongoing support they have given me during the writing of this book. First and foremost, I would like to thank my family, who educated me, taught me how to be independent and strong. Leonardo Mendes, who was the technical reviewer of this book and is one of my best friends. Gabriela Dias, who was the best leader that I had in these ten years of experience in IT and is a great example of a person for me. Juergen Bohn, the boss who brings me to Germany and opened so many doors and uncountable opportunities in Europe. I could have never completed this book without these people in my life.

This book wouldn't have happened if I hadn't had the support from BPB Publications, which gave me the support and attention while I was writing.

Finally, I would like to thank God who gave me the intelligence, strength and all the ways for me to be where I am right now.

Preface

DevOps was the most searched word in 2017. In my perspective, we can consider some revolution in IT when we stop creating boundaries among IT teams and start collaborating and working together, aiming for a common objective. Apart from that, we have all the technical stuff which are included in the DevOps mindset, using automation to speed up the time to market and delivery faster, high-quality software and services.

I came into DevOps because of my curiosity regarding everything in IT. I started when I was a teenager, studying cybersecurity, because I wanted to be a Hacker, like all geeks when they start with IT. Then I studied operating systems, computer programming, databases, network, security, etc. These terms prepareded me when DevOps came into the picture.

Today, the DevOps engineers must possess all these skills. In my daily work, for example, I have to create scripts to automate the cloud servers installation, which can be done in many different ways. Mostly, I use Python for my automation when it is something very specific. For more generic scenarios, I use Ansible. I use Jenkins for scheduling automation, creating pipelines, and many other tools.

I also wrote some other courses when I was living in Brazil, which included MongoDB, DevSecOps, Python Development, Docker and OpenShift, and Agile Infrastructure. In the ten years working there, I worked in different companies, in different scenarios, like web hosting, e-commerce development, open-source consultant, EdTech's, and payment gateways.

Today, my position is Big Data DevOps Engineer, wherein I apply my DevOps knowledge about automation into a Big Data scenario, to create pipelines, and automation to create data lakes, data pipelines, automating governance rules, etc.

The primary goal of this book is to provide the information and skills necessary to work in today's market as a DevOps Engineer, giving you the basic overview and steps of the most used technologies, based on my ten years of experience:

Chapter 1 This chapter introduces you with the the virtualization concept on your local machine aiming for you to create your labs, test your new technologies, simulate environments without crashing anything in production, and for your studying purposes.

Chapter 2 This chapter explains you about some basic bash commands, because we know that nowadays Linux is not a differential anymore, rather a requirement for those who work with Cloud and High Availability.

Chapter 3 Here, we set up some services, like a database and a web server bringing up the most common installation, what we call Lamp (Linux Apache Mysql PHP).

Chapter 4 Reverse proxy is commonly used when you have just one public IP, and you have different sites running behind a private structure. When you are not using cloud services, like Azure or Amazon, you can either set up your own Nginx and make the load balance, or you can pass your connections to the private servers enforcing the security.

Chapter 5 Docker is one of the leading technologies of a DevOps engineer stack. Here, we will learn the very basics, but enough for you to create your images and commit them to a registry for a deployment.

Chapter 6 Vagrant is also one very useful tool for those who are not using Docker yet. We know that many companies are still using on premise infrastructure. It also needs to be automated. Somehow, this chapter aims to teach you how to create your automation scripts.

Chapter 7 After working on your laptop, this chapter will teach you how to create the labs and infrastructure using Cloud Services and the CLI (Command-line interface), with a focus on automation.

Chapter 8 Multicloud is one topic that we cannot avoid. After learning the command-line interfaces and the differences among the different cloud providers, Terraform will give you a single workflow to create your infrastructure on any provider.

Chapter 9 At this point, we have created a lot of code. Therefore, we need to use Git to save it and also created documentation and different versions of our infrastructure.

Chapter 10 Pipelines is a way to create a workflow on your automation, defining dependencies, step-by-step, Jenkins is the most famous open source tool for it, and in this chapter, we will learn more about it.

Chapter 11 In my perspective, Kubernetes will become the standard way of application deployment, and then I could not write a book without giving you at least the basics of it.

Chapter 12 Once all your infrastructure is ready to be scaled and automated, we need to find a way to centralize the logs because when you have a few servers, you can go one-by-one and check the logs. But when we have planter thousands of servers, creating automated we must centralize the logs in the server for audition purposes and debugging, the Elasticsearch, Fluend, and Kibana are the references for it.

Downloading the coloured images:

Please follow the link to download the
Coloured Images of the book:

https://rebrand.ly/aeb0pwp

Errata

We take immense pride in our work at BPB Publications and follow best practices to ensure the accuracy of our content to provide with an indulging reading experience to our subscribers. Our readers are our mirrors, and we use their inputs to reflect and improve upon human errors, if any, that may have occurred during the publishing processes involved. To let us maintain the quality and help us reach out to any readers who might be having difficulties due to any unforeseen errors, please write to us at :

errata@bpbonline.com

Your support, suggestions and feedbacks are highly appreciated by the BPB Publications' Family.

Did you know that BPB offers eBook versions of every book published, with PDF and ePub files available? You can upgrade to the eBook version at www.bpbonline.com and as a print book customer, you are entitled to a discount on the eBook copy. Get in touch with us at :

business@bpbonline.com for more details.

At **www.bpbonline.com**, you can also read a collection of free technical articles, sign up for a range of free newsletters, and receive exclusive discounts and offers on BPB books and eBooks.

BPB is searching for authors like you

If you're interested in becoming an author for BPB, please visit **www.bpbonline.com** and apply today. We have worked with thousands of developers and tech professionals, just like you, to help them share their insight with the global tech community. You can make a general application, apply for a specific hot topic that we are recruiting an author for, or submit your own idea.

The code bundle for the book is also hosted on GitHub at **https://github. com/bpbpublications/Hands-on-DevOps-with-Linux**. In case there's an update to the code, it will be updated on the existing GitHub repository.

We also have other code bundles from our rich catalog of books and videos available at **https://github.com/bpbpublications**. Check them out!

PIRACY

If you come across any illegal copies of our works in any form on the internet, we would be grateful if you would provide us with the location address or website name. Please contact us at **business@bpbonline.com** with a link to the material.

If you are interested in becoming an author

If there is a topic that you have expertise in, and you are interested in either writing or contributing to a book, please visit **www.bpbonline.com**.

REVIEWS

Please leave a review. Once you have read and used this book, why not leave a review on the site that you purchased it from? Potential readers can then see and use your unbiased opinion to make purchase decisions, we at BPB can understand what you think about our products, and our authors can see your feedback on their book. Thank you!

For more information about BPB, please visit **www.bpbonline.com**.

Table of Contents

CHAPTER 1

Getting Started With Linux

This chapter will introduce you to the Linux world with a focus on servers. Therefore, I will not explain about it on desktops. You will see explanations about Linux, why you should know it, its basic concepts, and a lot of commands. I am a technical guy, so brace yourself because you are about to see how to set up your lab hands-on!

Structure

In this chapter, we will discuss the following topics:

- What is Linux
  - Distributions
  - Servers
- Setting up your environment
  - Installing the VirtualBox
  - Installing a Linux system
- Accessing via SSH
- Introduction to Bash
  - Useful commands
  - Basic files and how to edit them

      o Customizing your shell

      o Installing packages

Objectives

After studying this unit, you should be able to:

- Understand the basics of Linux
- Choose your favorite distribution
- Install your virtual machine
- Access any remote Linux server

What is Linux?

In my view, if you bought this book, you probably have a basic idea of what is Linux and you already know why you want to learn it. Thus summarizing, Linux is an operating system with an open-source code, and works similar to the famous Windows, but it does not belong to any company. So, how is the code open? Everyone can download the core Linux using this site: **https://www.kernel.org/**, and if you are interested to give a look around the source code, it can be found on this link **https://git.kernel.org/**.

Linux has this name because of its creator, *Linus Torvalds*. The first 3 letters are the initials of Linus, and the last 2 come from another OS, called Minix, created by a man, named *Andrew Tanenbaum*.

It is common for you to see Linux bound to other initials, like GNU. This happens because when *Linus Torvalds* was creating Linux, he used many tools that were created by the GNU project, **https://www.gnu.org/home.en.html**. The GNU project began with *Richard Stallman*, the creator of the Free Software Foundation, **https://www.fsf.org**. What does it mean to license an open-source? It means that every software written by the GNU project has its code open for everyone who wants to work on it. Then, how *Linus Torvalds* used the tools from the GNU project? He decided to use the same philosophy of the open-source and he released the Linux system with the tools from the GNU project. This explains the term GNU / Linux.

Distributions

Since Linux is open-source, a lot of people and companies created their own versions of Linux, which are called **distributions**. Everyone who has the knowledge in computer programming can make their own Linux distribution. One example is *Kurumin Linux,* created by a Brazilian programmer, Carlos Morimoto, and can be found on the link, **https://distrowatch.com/table.php?distribution=kurumin**. Unfortunately, it is discontinued, because maintaining your own distribution is not an easy task. You have to be concerned about updates, new releases, new software, bug correction, and infinite things that are basically impossible for just one person to take all that effort and without being paid for it. So, it is one important topic for you to decide what distribution you are planning to install in your infrastructure. Imagine the situation where you began with one distribution. A year later, it is discontinued and you have to reinstall your whole infrastructure with more than 300 servers. We, as professionals, cannot let this happen.

Regarding the distribution we want to choose for our infrastructure, there exists several of them, but some are the mostly used, because of the reasons I am going to explain further:

- **RedHat Enterprise Linux**: This is the most famous and corporative distribution because of the RedHat Company. It is one of the most famous companies in the Linux world. It has amazing support, frequent updates, and 100% compatibility with the RedHat software, like JBoss, OpenStack, RedHat Enterprise Virtualization Manager, and a lot of more options. But, for using RHEL, it is required to take a subscription with the company and pay for it. Otherwise, you will neither receive any updates, nor will you be able to access to the repository.

- **Community Enterprise Operating System**: CentOS is the community version of RHEL. It is the most common distribution among the companies that have chosen to not use the paid version and want to use the community version of the RedHat software.

- **SUSE**: It is the Novell (Microsoft) distribution and is a good option, because, Microsoft is one of the biggest companies around the world. Therefore, the probability of it being discontinued is zero, and you will always have the updates and new software published by the company. It also has a community version called the OpenSUSE which follows the same features of the CentOS.

- **Debian**: This is the option for those who are more involved in the community and do not want to be bound to any company, like the distros mentioned previously. Debian is 100% maintained by the community and is one of the oldest distros we have. Also running over a lot of servers, it is very stable and reliable, and is frequently used by the companies and common users.

- **Ubuntu**: This distro was made in Africa by Canonical that used to distribute CDs over the whole world for people to get to know more about Linux and run it on their desktops. The final users were the target by Canonical in the beginning. So, I believe that for desktops, Ubuntu is the most used distro, and for servers, it is CentOS. Ubuntu has a version for server which is my favorite distribution. That's why I am writing this book using Ubuntu. But the knowledge you will acquire here can be used for all the distributions.

Servers

Servers are nothing more than computers. They are usually more powerful than PCs, which are created and installed to attend to a purpose. For example, we can install a Linux server for acting, like web server. In other words, to run a website on it, like Facebook, Amazon, or Google. It can also act like a database server where we can install a PostgreSQL, SQL Server, MySQL, Oracle, or another that can be fileserver where the company stores all the data inside it, and in many cases, all of it together. One example of it is what we call the LAMP, Linux Apache MySQL PHP. Usually, we call a server LAMP when we have a Linux system (a webserver, in that case), Apache, a database server (MySQL), and a programming language interpreter, in this case, PHP. We can also call this a stack. Stack means a set of tools that you can use to solve a problem. One of my favorite stacks is NPM, Nginx, Python, and MongoDB. I have been using it to solve many issues in the company that I work. This stack can be installed in a server, which can be virtual or physical, and we will do that in the next chapters.

On-premise is a term often used for server installed within the infrastructure of our companies, many-a-times, in a datacenter, and sometimes, under the system admin desk. The VMs can also run in an on-premise infrastructure when we use tools like OpenStack or oVirt to create them on the top of physical servers. It is a strategy adopted by the companies towards having more resilience, flexibility, and better use of our resources. One example is if you have to switch one or more servers in your datacenter, for the fact that it is very old and is not able to have the same performance as the other servers, you can migrate the VMs from one server to another. Switch the physical machine and after installing a new one, migrate all the VMs back.

Cloud is the name used to describe when the virtual servers are installed inside the infrastructure of something else. In most cases, the companies like AWS, Azure, and GCP have their own on-premise infrastructure and rent it for us. So, we do not need to take care of the maintenance, like switching disks when they fail, switching the server when they are deprecated, or even the electricity and the internet. Furthermore, you can save costs by turning them off after the business day and starting them again the next day. All these providers only charge you for the time that the machine is turned on. Otherwise, you are going to pay only for the storage.

Conclusion

Now that we already have a brief explanation regarding the servers, virtual machines, Linux, and distributions, we are ready to start the hands-on. Let's begin by setting up our first Linux environment and get to know the basics, and so much more.

Setting up your environment

One of the most important tasks for a Linux professional is the skill to set up different types of environment, run web server, databases, file systems, and many different services by different vendors. In this chapter, we will see where to download a Linux distribution from, how to install a virtualization tool to create your testing environments, how to create a base image to make it easier for the creation of new labs, and if you crash your testing environment, what happens very often when we learn new stuff.

To run VMs on your laptop or personal computer, you need to check if your processor arch is 64-bit. This specification can be found at the laptop manufacturer or processor manufacturer. After checking this setting, you need to enable virtualization at your device's BIOS or UEFI. This configuration can be very different according to your equipment, but in most of the cases, it can be found in the **Advanced** or **Security** option with the name Intel Virtualization Technology.

Installing the VirtualBox

Nowadays, we have many options for virtualization tools to run on your laptop, like VMware Player, KVM, QEMU, HyperV. But, in my opinion, VirtualBox is the easiest one and has all the features we need to create our labs.

To install the VirtualBox, you need to download its latest version from the official website:

https://www.virtualbox.org/wiki/Downloads

I am using Windows system, so, I am going to download the Windows version. But, if you have the basic knowledge of Linux or you are using MacOS, the steps are basically the same.

After downloading the file, double click and the installation step is basically **Next**, **Next**, and **Finish**. The following first window is just explaining that you are about to install the VirtualBox:

Figure 1.1

The second window is important for you to select all the resources, because a lot of times, they are needed mainly when you want to share the files between your PC and the VM, or even configure networks:

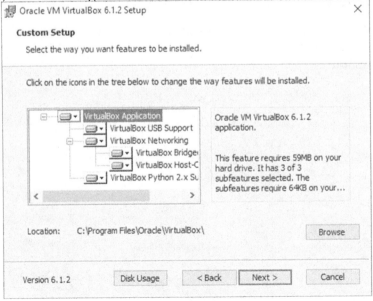

Figure 1.2

Following are the basic options about the shortcuts, if you want to add them to your desktop:

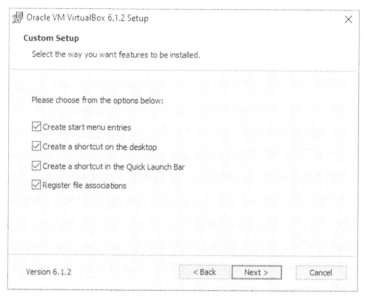

Figure 1.3

At this step, the installation will ask you for the **Admin Rights,** because the VirtualBox will create a **bridge interface.** This interface is responsible for the communication between the host machine and the VM, and without it, you will not be able to access the internet from your virtual machine:

Figure 1.4

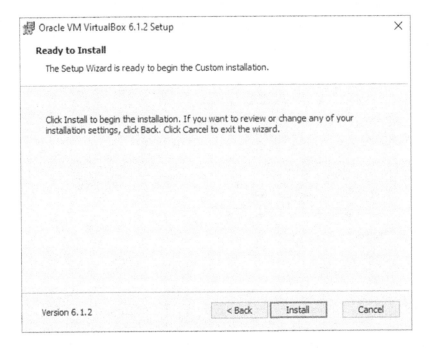

Figure 1.5

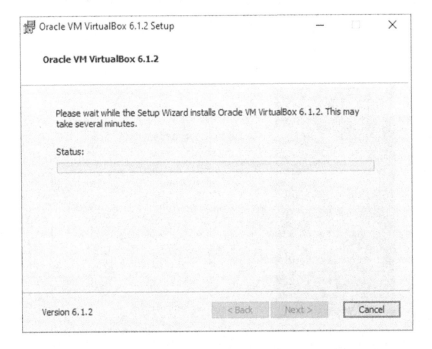

Figure 1.6

After the installation completes, you will be able to open the VirtualBox, and the main screen will be as shown in the following figure:

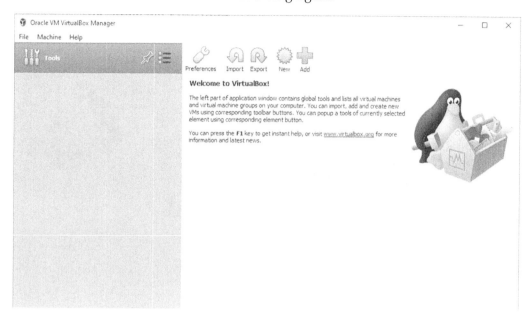

Figure 1.7

Now, we are ready to set up our first Linux environment. The VirtualBox has a lot of options for you to configure and explore. But, I will not focus on it now because we have a Linux system to install.

Installing the Linux System

Since I mentioned earlier that we will use the Ubuntu server to do everything in this book, you can download the latest version from this link:

https://ubuntu.com/download/server

Then, download this file: `ubuntu-18.04.3-live-server-amd64.iso`

Now, let's start the installation. The first step is to open the VirtualBox, click on **New**, and in the new window, type **UbuntuServer**, as given in the following example:

Oracle VM VirtualBox Manager
File Machine Help
Tools
Preferences Import Export New Add
Create Virtual Machine
Name and operating system
Please choose a descriptive name and destination folder for the new virtual machine and select the type of operating system you intend to install on it. The name you choose will be used throughout VirtualBox to identify this machine.
Name: UbuntuServer
Machine Folder: D:\VirtualBox VMs
Type: Linux
Version: Ubuntu (64-bit)
Expert Mode
Next
Cancel

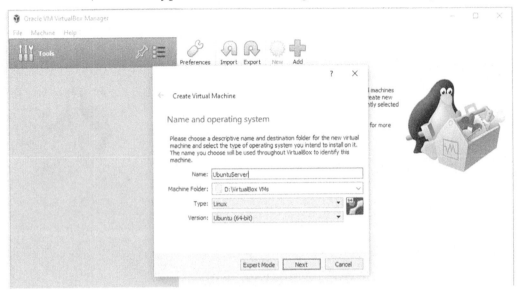

Figure 1.8

After clicking on **Next,** you need to define the amount of memory you want to have in your VM. The Linux system, usually, does not need a lot of memory to work, but, after you install your services and test them, you will need more memory. For now, 1 GB is enough. Then, click on **Next**:

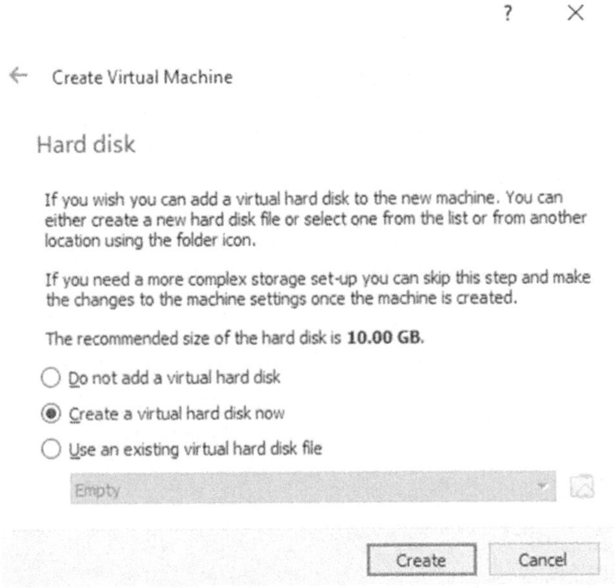

Create Virtual Machine
Hard disk
If you wish you can add a virtual hard disk to the new machine. You can either create a new hard disk file or select one from the list or from another location using the folder icon.
If you need a more complex storage set-up you can skip this step and make the changes to the machine settings once the machine is created.
The recommended size of the hard disk is 10.00 GB.
Do not add a virtual hard disk
Create a virtual hard disk now
Use an existing virtual hard disk file
Empty
Create
Cancel

Figure 1.9

In this part, create a **New Disk.** The disk is basically a file in your disk where the VM will store all the data. Click on **Create** and you will see the following window:

Figure 1.10

VDI is the standard type used by the VirtualBox. You can change the type if you intend to import this machine in other Virtualization Tool. **VMDK**, for example, is the type used by VMware. Click on **Next**:

Figure 1.11

This window is very important. In your laboratories, you will always use the **Dynamically allocated** option, because the VirtualBox will create a small file and will increase the size according to the disk usage.

The **Fixed Size** is recommended for the production environments, because the Virtualization Tool will reserve that space for your VM. Even if you don't use all the disk space allocated, it will avoid you from having more Virtual Space than the **Physical Space.** In some cases, when you use the **Dynamically allocated** size in production environments, you overcome the total space of your **Storage,** but your virtual machines still have free space. I had experienced this in the past and it is really hard to deal with. One more reason to choose this option is because you avoid your Virtualization Tool to recalculate the disk space after every writes. When you use the **Dynamically allocated** type for every write, your system will calculate the actual size and how much it needs to increase before it reaches the defined limit:

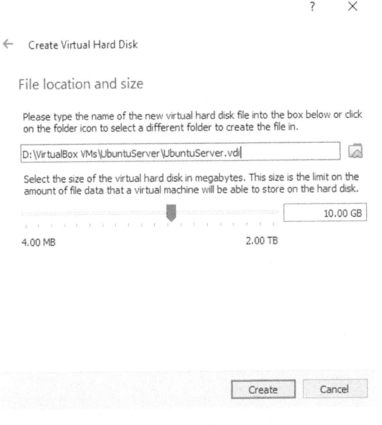

Figure 1.12

Here, you can define where the VM data will be stored and the disk size. For us, 10 GB is enough to run our tests:

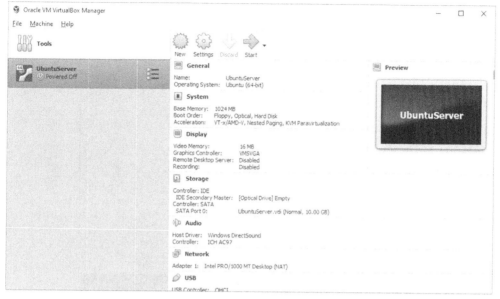

Figure 1.13

Now, your VM is created!

Installing Your Linux System

Once we have all the prerequisites, like creating the VM and defining all the configurations, it's time to install the system. So, double click on your VM. The following screen will sppear:

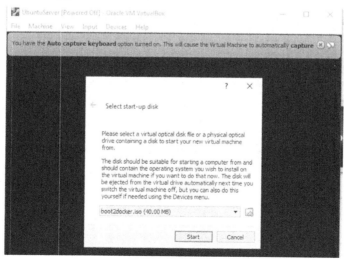

Figure 1.14

You do not have any operating system installed in this VM. You need to select the ISO download from the Ubuntu website by clicking on the yellow folder:

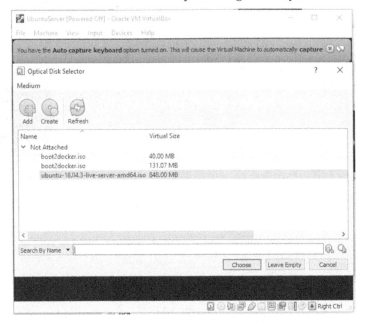

Figure 1.15

Click on **Add**, and select the ISO file you had already downloaded. Select it, click on choose, and **Start**:

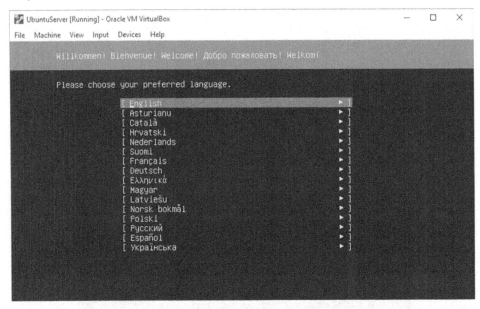

Figure 1.16

Now, select your language. I always select **English** even when I lived in Brazil, Canada, and now in Germany. Selecting this option, for sure, will avoid a lot of problems regarding collation, like punctuation, special characters, etc.:

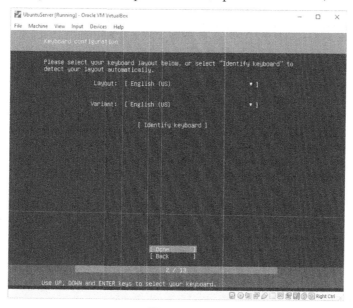

Figure 1.17

This option depends on your keyboard layout. You will probably need to change it according to the country you are living in the moment. My keyboard has the layout of the US, so I will select this option:

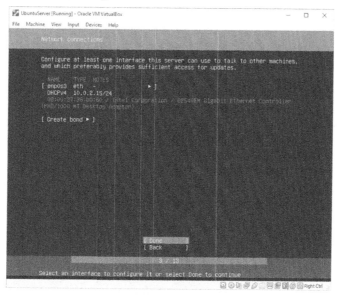

Figure 1.18

Now, you don't need to do anything. Just press **Done**, because we will use the default configuration. This step is really important because Ubuntu will download some updates during the installation. So, it is important to have an internet connection in your PC and in your VM:

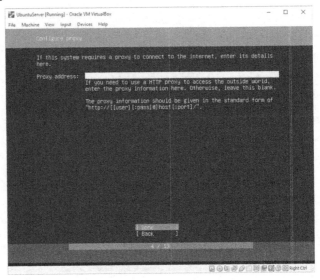

Figure 1.19

If you are doing this during your work time, and if your company has the proxy to access the internet, now is the time for you to configure. So, just put the proxy URL and press **Done**:

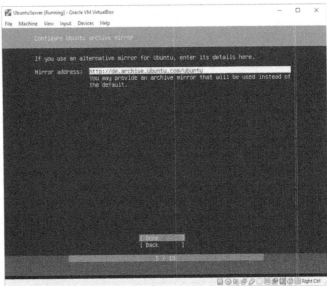

Figure 1.20

Here, you can define the Mirror where Ubuntu will download the updates. If you have an internet connection, it will select the nearest mirror to you. In my case, I have the German repository:

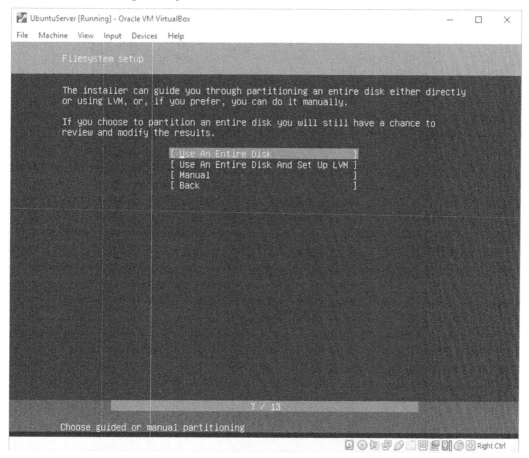

Figure 1.21

Years ago, I would have given you a big explanation about the important directories on Linux, which is the best way to split your disk among the directories and the partitions. But nowadays, it is not that important when we work with the virtual machines. We can consider the Amazon EC2 instances as an example. These do not even have the SWAP partition. If you lack space, just increase more in your root partition and clean your server. Another important thing is the /var directory. I won't go deep into that topic now, but it is the directory where the logs of your Linux system are stored. Therefore, they frequently use a lot of your free space and we have to clean it often. Years ago, I would ask you split it into a different partition.

But today, we have tools to ship the logs to a **Log Server**, and we can just remove the logs every day from the local machine. However, select **Use An Entire Disk**:

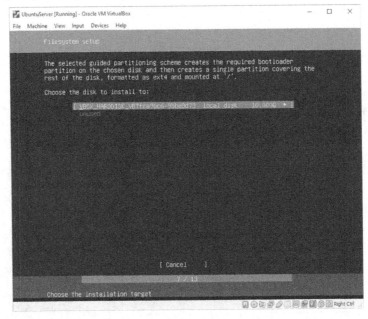

Figure 1.22

Now, select the physical device where the operating system will be installed, and press *Enter*:

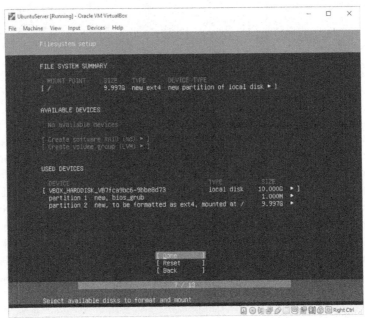

Figure 1.23

The following screen shows you how your disk has been partitioned. We can see that there is a **Physical Device**, VBOX_HARDDISK, and it is split into two parts. The boot partition, which is mandatory to boot your system, is where the bootloader is installed.

The root partition, also known as /. Just select **Done**:

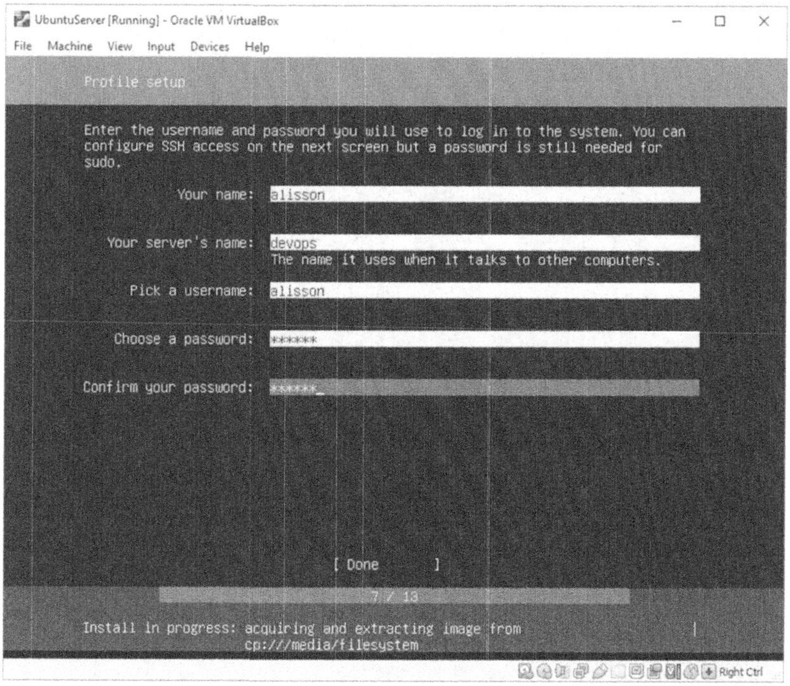

Figure 1.24

Here, we will create the first user, and then I will define the following data:

- Your name: alisson - this is just your real name, but it will not be used for anything.
- Your Server's name: devops - this is the hostname of your machine
- Pick a username: alisson - this is literally the user which you will use to access the server
- Choose a password: devops
- Confirm your password: devops

Press **Done**.

Attention!

The following step is really important. The OpenSSH server is not installed by default, so you have to select the option, and install the OpenSSH server. You can use the key *Tab* to change the options. Otherwise, you will not be able to access your server from a remote connection:

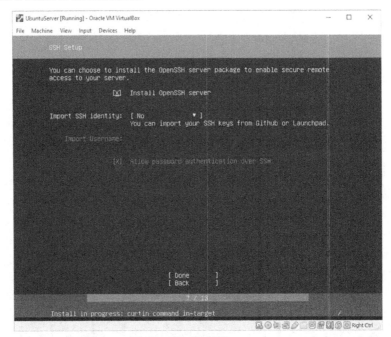

Figure 1.25

Now that you have selected the right option, press **Done**:

Figure 1.26

Now, you need to select a **Template** of installation for your server, like a Nextcloud server. Or, if you intend to run Kubernetes, you can select the **microk8s**, But it is not what we want. So, press *Tab* to change the option to **Done**, and press *Enter*:

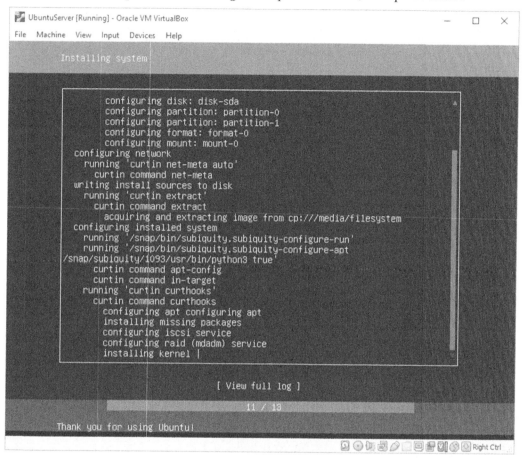

Figure 1.27

Now, your installation has begun. It may take a while because Ubuntu will download the updates and some important packages. You are not obligated to do the updates. But, in my view, it is important for those who are learning Linux to have an updated system. Just wait for the installation to finish, and when Ubuntu asks you for a **Reboot**, do that. After the reboot, you will see the following screen:

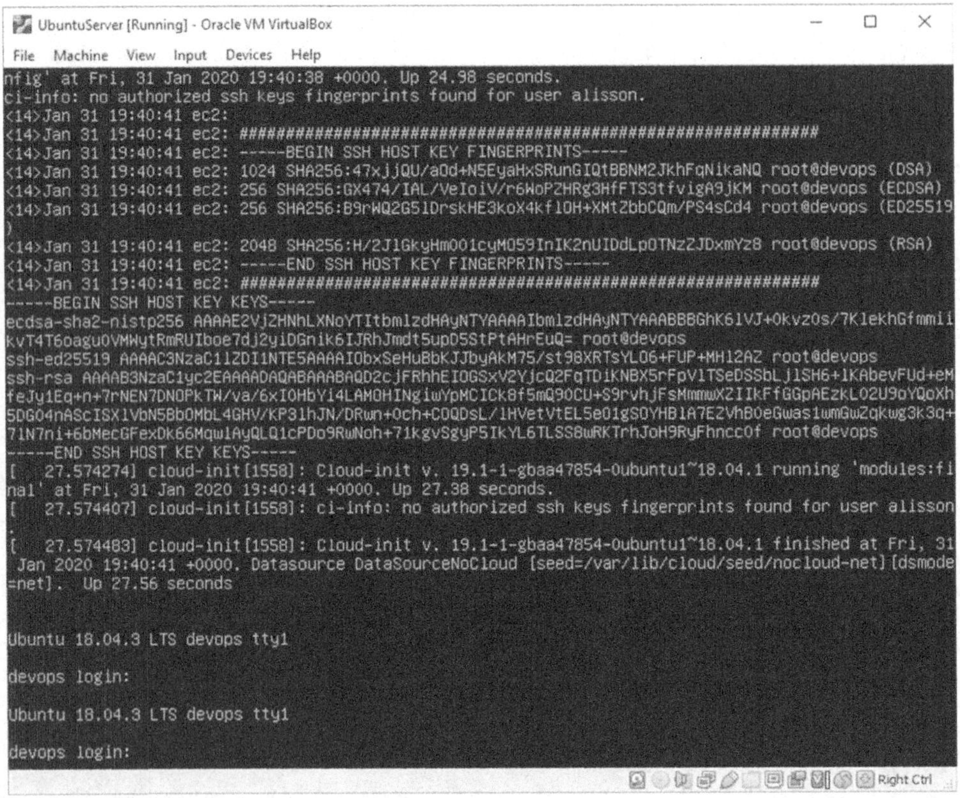

Figure 1.28

Enter the credentials defined during your installation:

```
login: alisson
password: devops
```

Now, you are inside the Linux shell. Starting now, you will be able to run the commands, install packages, and do everything that you want with your server. This access console is exactly what you would do if you were inside a datacenter. Plug a **KVM (Keyboard Video Mouse)** to a server and run the commands. I did a lot of that when I was working with Colocation. This is a business model in which you can buy your own physical servers and install inside the datacenter of someone else's. Thus, you will use the datacenter infrastructure, but the server belongs to you.

It is not used much, unless you are working within a datacenter. If you are still logged in into your machine, run the following command:

```
ip a
```

The preceding command will show all the network interfaces you have and their IP address, like the following screenshot:

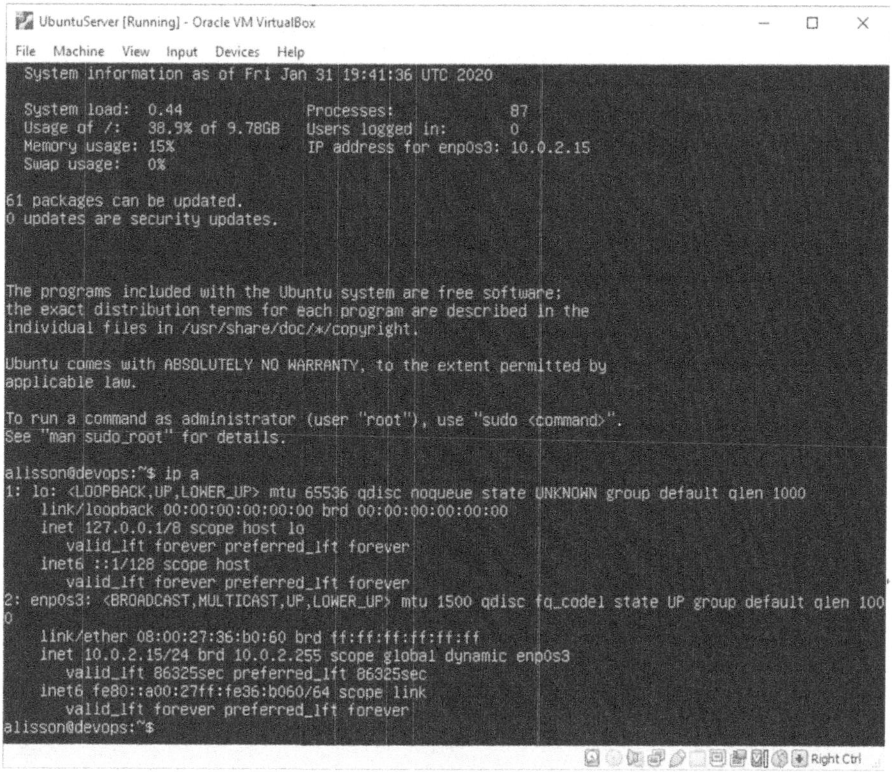

Figure 1.29

We just have 2 IP addresses and 2 interfaces:

`Interface: lo`

`IP Address: 127.0.0.1`

This is the local IP address. It is used to make the TCP/IP connection without getting outside of the machine:

`Interface: enp0s3`

`IP Address: 10.0.2.15`

This is a NAT interface. We need this interface just to make the internet connection. But, we cannot access the machine from outside using this configuration. It is used just for the installation purposes. We could have changed that before. However, I wanted to show you how to change that configuration and why we need to do it.

To change this configuration, go to the main screen of the VirtualBox. Now, click on the virtual machine, and then, click on **Settings** | **Network**. In this part, **Attached**, you will see the value Nat. Change it to the **Bridge Network**, and in the option **Name**: select the network interface that you have the internet access to. In my case, it is configured like the following screenshot:

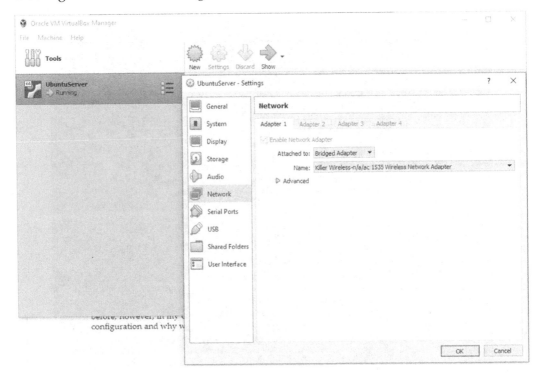

Figure 1.30

After saving the configuration, go back to your VM and run the following command again:

```
ip a
```

You will see a new IP address. In my case,**192.168.178.62** was attached:

```
alisson@devops:~$ ip a
1: lo: <LOOPBACK,UP,LOWER_UP> mtu 65536 qdisc noqueue state UNKNOWN group default qlen 1000
    link/loopback 00:00:00:00:00:00 brd 00:00:00:00:00:00
    inet 127.0.0.1/8 scope host lo
       valid_lft forever preferred_lft forever
    inet6 ::1/128 scope host
       valid_lft forever preferred_lft forever
2: enp0s3: <BROADCAST,MULTICAST,UP,LOWER_UP> mtu 1500 qdisc fq_codel state UP group default qlen 100
0
    link/ether 08:00:27:36:b0:60 brd ff:ff:ff:ff:ff:ff
    inet 192.168.178.62/24 brd 192.168.178.255 scope global dynamic enp0s3
       valid_lft 863999sec preferred_lft 863999sec
    inet6 fe80::a00:27ff:fe36:b060/64 scope link
       valid_lft forever preferred_lft forever
alisson@devops:~$ _
```

Figure 1.31

Accessing via SSH

We have a connection from the outside now. So, how can we connect to that machine using the SSH? In the past, it was common to use tools like Putty to SSH the servers from Windows machines, but in the new versions of Windows, we have PowerShell, which is installed by default and we can use it to access our VM.

Open the PowerShell if you're using Windows or Terminal in Linux/MacOS, and run the following command:

`ssh alisson@192.168.178.62`

The command follows the structure USER@HOSTNAME. If you do not have a hostname configured, you can use the IP address. After that, press *Enter*. It will show you the following message:

```
The authenticity of host '192.168.178.62 (192.168.178.62)' can't be
established.
```

```
ECDSA key fingerprint is SHA256:GX474/IAL/VeIoiV/
r6WoPZHRg3HfFTS3tfvigA9jKM.
```

```
Are you sure you want to continue connecting (yes/no)? yes
```

```
Warning: Permanently added '192.168.178.62' (ECDSA) to the list of known
hosts.
```

It happens because this is the first time you are connecting to that server. You can just type Yes to make sure that you want to connect to it and then, the SSH will ask for your password:

`alisson@192.168.178.62's password:`

Type the password defined in your installation. In my case, it was DevOps, and you will be able to access the Linux shell again:

```
Welcome to Ubuntu 18.04.3 LTS (GNU/Linux 4.15.0-76-generic x86_64)
Welcome to Ubuntu 18.04.3 LTS (GNU/Linux 4.15.0-76-generic x86_64)


* Documentation:  https://help.ubuntu.com

* Management:     https://landscape.canonical.com

* Support:        https://ubuntu.com/advantage


System information as of Fri Jan 31 20:04:07 UTC 2020


System load:  0.0                Processes:            88

Usage of /:   39.0% of 9.78GB    Users logged in:      1
```

```
Memory usage: 15%                    IP address for enp0s3: 192.168.178.62
Swap usage:   0%


61 packages can be updated.
0 updates are security updates.


Last login: Fri Jan 31 19:41:36 2020
To run a command as administrator (user "root"), use "sudo <command>".
See "man sudo_root" for details.


alisson@devops:~$
```

There is a lot of theory and concepts about the SSH connections which are encrypted, and we have the known_hosts files. It is important to know if you want to become a Linux expert, but not that important for us now.

We know that using a password to access the server is not the best practice, because they are a lot reliable and are easily exposed. So, we can create a key pair to secure our access. You can exit from your shell by typing the following command:

```
alisson@devops:~$ logout
Connection to 192.168.178.62 closed.
```

Or press *Ctrl + D*. In your PowerShell console, type the following command:

ssh-keygen

And press *Enter* for all the options. This command will generate two files for you:

- id_rsa: id_rsa is your private key. This should be in your PC, and only you can have this file.
- id_rsa.pub: id_rsa.pub is the public key. You will copy this file to every Linux server you want to access without a password.

To copy your public key to our server, run the following command:

```
scp .\.ssh\id_rsa.pub alisson@192.168.178.62:/home/alisson/id_rsa.pub
alisson@192.168.178.62's password:
id_rsa.pub
100%  398    397.4KB/s    00:00
```

The file was copied, so access the server again:

ssh alisson@192.168.178.62

```
alisson@192.168.178.62's password:
```

Create the .ssh directory and create the authorized_keys file. This file will store all the public keys to access the server using the user alisson:

mkdir .ssh

cat id_rsa.pub >> .ssh/authorized_keys

logout

Now, if you try to access the server again, no password will be asked, like the following example:

ssh alisson@192.168.178.62

```
Welcome to Ubuntu 18.04.3 LTS (GNU/Linux 4.15.0-76-generic x86_64)Welcome
to Ubuntu 18.04.3 LTS (GNU/Linux 4.15.0-76-generic x86_64)


* Documentation:  https://help.ubuntu.com

* Management:     https://landscape.canonical.com

* Support:        https://ubuntu.com/advantage


System information as of Fri Jan 31 20:24:51 UTC 2020


System load:   0.2            Processes:              88
Usage of /:    39.0% of 9.78GB Users logged in:        1
Memory usage: 15%             IP address for enp0s3: 192.168.178.62
Swap usage:    0%


61 packages can be updated.
0 updates are security updates.


Last login: Fri Jan 31 20:20:28 2020 from 192.168.178.60
To run a command as administrator (user "root"), use "sudo <command>".
See "man sudo_root" for details.


alisson@devops:~$
```

Mission complete! Now we are ready to learn more about the Bash, directories, files, and many more.

Conclusion

This was just the first chapter with the basics on how to install your own Linux server, and create your labs on the top of the VirtualBox. I strongly recommend you to do all these steps again using other Linux distributions and discover which one is your favorite. When I started using Linux, I created my own labs using different distributions, including Slackware, Gentoo, BigLinux, Mandrake, Mandriva. So, feel free to choose your own. In the companies I worked for all these years, most of them used RedHat or CentOS, and they had theirs on on-premises infrastructure. But, since I started to work with Cloud, it has been changing. If you try to create Ubuntu server machine on Amazon, you will see that it is one of the most used distributions.

CHAPTER 2
Working with Bash

This chapter will explain the basics for you to navigate inside your Linux system, the main directories, mostly used commands, important files, managing users and groups, and how the Linux permission system works!

Structure

In this chapter, we will discuss the following topics:

- What is Bash?
    - Introduction
    - Basic commands
- Managing files and directories
    - Structure of directories
    - Important files
    - Customizing your environment
- Managing users and groups
    - Creating and modifying users
    - Creating and modifying groups

- Working with permissions
  - o Changing read and write permissions
  - o Changing the owner of files and executing scripts

Objectives

After studying this unit, you should be able to:

- Understand directories infrastructure
- Customize your environment using important files
- Manage users and groups
- Understand the permissions and executing scripts

What is Bash?

Bash is an abbreviation of Bourne Again Shell. It is an improved version of the Legacy Shell that we used to see in older Linux/Unix Systems. In this version, we have many features, like creating functions, controlling jobs in the foreground and background, creating aliases, customizing your environment, putting color in your terminal, new shortcuts, auto-complete, and many other features that we are going to see in this chapter. Just to give you more context about it, Shell is the interface on Linux which is used to administer the system. In other words, it is where we run all the commands.

It is also a programming language. Often among Linux users, we see the term Shell Scripting. What does it mean? It means we can get all the commands used during our work, put all of them together in the same file, give permission to execute it, and automate your daily job. It is a Shell Script. It is basically the Swiss Knife of the Linux administrators. Today, it is frequently challenged by Python, because Python is an object-oriented language and has a lot of features which are very easy to use if we compare it with the Shell Script. Nevertheless, it will always be the favorite tool of all the Linux administrators to automate easy tasks, and at the end of this chapter, I will teach how to create a script using all the commands learned before.

Introduction

In the last chapter, we configured and installed our Linux system and we were able to access it using the SSH tool. The point where we stopped is as follows:

```
ssh alisson@192.168.178.62

Welcome to Ubuntu 18.04.3 LTS (GNU/Linux 4.15.0-76-generic x86_64)
```

```
* Documentation:  https://help.ubuntu.com
* Management:      https://landscape.canonical.com
* Support:        https://ubuntu.com/advantage

System information disabled due to load higher than 1.0

* Multipass 1.0 is out! Get Ubuntu VMs on demand on your Linux, Windows
or

Mac. Supports cloud-init for fast, local, cloud devops simulation.

https://multipass.run/

60 packages can be updated.
6 updates are security updates.

Last login: Mon Feb 10 18:59:46 2020
To run a command as administrator (user "root"), use "sudo <command>".
See "man sudo_root" for details.

alisson@devops:~$
```

It means we are inside the Linux Shell. Now, we are going to call it Bash because it is the command-line interpreter used. Every operating system has its own command-line interpreter, because it is required to administer the system. In the older versions of Windows, we had MS-DOS. Now, we have the PowerShell. In the older versions of Linux, we had the Shell. Now, we have the Bash and some users are migrating from Bash to Z shell. I will show in the following pages how we can change our **CLI (Command Line Interpreter)**.

Within your server, the most useful command is called ls:

```
alisson@devops:~$ ls

id_rsa.pub
```

This command is used to show the files and the directories of Linux. It can be used with different parameters. For example, if I want to show the files and directories in a detailed mode, I can pass the parameter –l:

```
alisson@devops:~$ ls -l

total 4

-rw-rw-r-- 1 alisson alisson 398 Jan 31 20:18 id_rsa.pub

alisson@devops:~$
```

The last output shows us more information following that sequence:

```
Permissions - Number of the Hard Links - User - Group - Size - Last
Modification Date - Filename
```

This kind of information is called the metadata. But why does it have this name? Because, we have a file which contains the data that we use, and this data is about the file that is used the most by the OS. For example, we need not always know the size of a file, but the operating system always needs that kind of information, because it needs to calculate the free and used space on the disk.

If you want to see more about the metadata of a file, use the following command stat:

```
alisson@devops:~$ stat id_rsa.pub
File: id_rsa.pub
Size: 398              Blocks: 8          IO Block: 4096    regular file
Device: 802h/2050d      Inode: 532800       Links: 1
Access: (0664/-rw-rw-r--) Uid: ( 1000/ alisson)   Gid: ( 1000/ alisson)
Access: 2020-01-31 20:20:23.741638861 +0000
Modify: 2020-01-31 20:18:39.467733742 +0000
Change: 2020-01-31 20:18:39.467733742 +0000
Birth: -
```

This command will show you all the metadata about the file and in a detailed form.

One very interesting parameter of the ls is the -a, which will show you all the files including the hidden ones. In Linux, all the hidden files starts with a . (dot) in the beginning. For example:

```
alisson@devops:~$ ls -la
total 40
drwxr-xr-x 5 alisson alisson 4096 Jan 31 20:20 .
drwxr-xr-x 3 root    root    4096 Jan 31 19:40 ..
-rw------- 1 alisson alisson  113 Jan 31 20:20 .bash_history
-rw-r--r-- 1 alisson alisson  220 Apr  4  2018 .bash_logout
-rw-r--r-- 1 alisson alisson 3771 Apr  4  2018 .bashrc
drwx------ 2 alisson alisson 4096 Jan 31 19:41 .cache
drwx------ 3 alisson alisson 4096 Jan 31 19:41 .gnupg
-rw-rw-r-- 1 alisson alisson  398 Jan 31 20:18 id_rsa.pub
-rw-r--r-- 1 alisson alisson  807 Apr  4  2018 .profile
drwxrwxr-x 2 alisson alisson 4096 Jan 31 20:20 .ssh
```

We can see a lot of files now, like the .bashrc or .bash_history or the hidden directory .ssh, which we used in the first chapter to save our public key to access the server without any password.

If you want to see the content of a file, you can use the command cat:

alisson@devops:~$ **cat .bash_logout**

~/.bash_logout: executed by bash(1) when login shell exits.

when leaving the console clear the screen to increase privacy

if ["$SHLVL" = 1]; then
[-x /usr/bin/clear_console] && /usr/bin/clear_console -q
fi

Using the command cat, we were able to see the content of the .bash_logout file. This file has some importance, because if we want to execute a command before logging out of the server, we should put in this file.

To display a message on the screen, use the command echo:

alisson@devops:~$ **echo Message on Terminal**

Message on Terminal

This command is often used to create a file as well:

alisson@devops:~$ **echo Creating a file > message.txt**

alisson@devops:~$ **ls**

id_rsa.pub message.txt

alisson@devops:~$ **cat message.txt**

Creating a file

> **We can use redirectors at Shell Script to send command outputs to write the files. There exist many redirectors, but the most used are ">" and ">>".**
>
> **If you use ">" after a command, the standard output of the command is redirected to a file that you need to specify. But, if you select an existing file, the redirector will overwrite it.**
>
> **If you use ">>" after a command, the standard output of the command is redirected to a file that you need to specify too. But, if you select an existing file, the redirector will append it and not overwrite it.**

To manage files, most commands use the same syntax. If you want to copy, move, or rename a file, you can use COMMAND <SOURCE FILE><DESTINATION FILE>.

Renaming a file:

```
alisson@devops:~$ mv message.txt file.txt

alisson@devops:~$ ls

file.txt   id_rsa.pub
```

Copying a file:

```
alisson@devops:~$ cp file.txt file2.txt

alisson@devops:~$ ls

file2.txt   file.txt   id_rsa.pub
```

In the first chapter, we edited a file and called authorized_keys. If we want to check this file again, we can access the directory using the command cd:

```
alisson@devops:~$ cd .ssh/

alisson@devops:~/.ssh$ ls

authorized_keys
```

And, we can check the file content again:

```
alisson@devops:~/.ssh$ cat authorized_keys

ssh-rsa AAAAB3NzaC1yc2EAAAADAQABAAAABAQChi8HX26xv9Rk9gz47Qhb+Tu7MRqGIyP
xnheIeEgFad/dlqG4w4pY7y5dtx5LNGE9C01varco5dZagqsHplI7M+5ECSvjAuS6b5r
kYZwZiZruDXxckcQHFpr2yIz 3DOzKRTUc5Hg5JHF5aymiqyVfTsxL/aI/LDY8Ikh+
INn3S9+b5bZtU+74tA6yuqt h5SCtNSWwMUlv7QL6ONHtQiviAjBe+ksDBBV6thWz2ZIJA/
jApSIBJWK9AWmZwq 2hFy9sOZArUDB2Kt6kl3rIZnHpqJ/GMUCxFhtggYamJ5J2H62
77qLFqLZ/8tum9uc5l/1SWYKTDm2+E/prQfmFrxPf9 1511 mxti@avell
```

If you need to know the directory you are working on, use the following command:

```
alisson@devops:~/.ssh$ pwd

/home/alisson/.ssh
```

And if you want to go to the previous directory again, use the command cd using two dots (. .):

```
alisson@devops:~/.ssh$ cd ..

alisson@devops:~$ pwd

/home/alisson
```

Managing files and directories

After getting to know some basic commands, it is really important for you to know how to navigate among the directories, know the files within them, and what we can do using these files. So, now we will see what the root directory is, where the configuration files are, what these files do for our Linux system, and how we can customize the environment using it.

Structure of directories

To see the basic structure of the directories on Linux, use the following command:

```
alisson@devops:~$ ls /
bin    cdrom  etc    initrd.img       lib      lost+found  mnt   proc  run
snap   swap.img tmp  var              vmlinuz.old

boot   dev    home   initrd.img.old   lib64    media             opt   root  sbin
srv    sys           usr  vmlinuz
```

Here, we have some directories. I will explain just the most important of them:

- **/:** It is the root directory and everything that runs in your Linux system is below this directory.

- **/etc:** This directory stores all the configuration files on Linux.

- **/var:** This directory stores the log files and data of some services. For example, if you have a MySQL server installed in your system, you can find all the data stored inside `/var/lib/mysql/data`.

- **/lib:** Here you will find the libraries of your system. We do not have to often access this directory, but it is an important one to know. For example, the kernel modules are stored in `/lib/modules`.

- **/bin:** This directory stores the binaries. In other words, the programs are required for your Linux Words. For example, the command `ls`, it is found in this directory.

- **/usr:** Here you can find some binaries, like the `/bin`. But the binaries installed here are not required for your system works. For example, `/usr/bin/at`, this binary allows you to schedule a task to run in your system, but you can live without that.

- **/boot:** In this directory, you can find your kernel installed. My current version is: `/boot/vmlinuz-4.15.0-76-generic`.

- **/proc:** This is the current process running. One fact about this directory is it only exists when your Linux is turned on. If you have a dual boot and you try to mount your Linux partition, you will be able to see all the directories, except the `/proc`, because it is your RAM content.

- **/opt:** Usually, it becomes empty after your installation. But, when you compile a program, it is a good practice to put the binaries and the configuration files in this directory.

- **/sbin:** This is exactly like the /bin, but the binaries here require administration permissions. For example, if you want to format a partition, you will call the command /sbin/fdisk. You cannot run this command as a common user.

- **/home:** In this directory, you will find the home directory of all the common users. The only exception is the user root; its home directory can be found in /root.

- **/mnt:** Here, you can use to mount network shares; your pendrive, SD card, and another kind of external volumes.

These are the most important directories you can find in your Linux system and they will be a part of your daily work.

Important Files

Now that you already know the important directories, let's get inside of them and see the files that are important for our system to work.

One important file is the /etc/passwd. This file is responsible to store all the Linux users, and we can give a look at its content using the cat command:

```
alisson@devops:~$ cat /etc/passwd
root:x:0:0:root:/root:/bin/bash
daemon:x:1:1:daemon:/usr/sbin:/usr/sbin/nologin
bin:x:2:2:bin:/bin:/usr/sbin/nologin
sys:x:3:3:sys:/dev:/usr/sbin/nologin
sync:x:4:65534:sync:/bin:/bin/sync
```

This was an example of the first 5 lines. Its structure follows the following sequence:

```
User - password - user id - group id - comment - home folder - shell
```

The data is separated by a colon (:). It is important to know that the Linux shell has many useful commands to work with these kinds of files.

For example, we could use the command cut to see just the information we want:

```
alisson@devops:~$ cut -f 1,6,7 -d : /etc/passwd
root:/root:/bin/bash
daemon:/usr/sbin:/usr/sbin/nologin
bin:/bin:/usr/sbin/nologin
sys:/dev:/usr/sbin/nologin
```

Thus, in the example, I printed just the columns 1, 6, 7 which correspond to the user, the home folder, and the shell.

I am not posting the entire output of the command because I want to save some space. But, you probably are running this on your own virtual machine. So, if you want to show just the first 3 lines of any file, you can use the command head. By default, this command shows the first 10 lines of a file, but we have the -n parameter, where we can define as many lines we want to see.

For example:

```
alisson@devops:~$ head -n 3 /etc/passwd
root:x:0:0:root:/root:/bin/bash
daemon:x:1:1:daemon:/usr/sbin:/usr/sbin/nologin
bin:x:2:2:bin:/bin:/usr/sbin/nologin
```

On Linux, it is also possible to concatenate the commands. If you want to see just the first 3 lines and only the columns 1, 6, 7 like we did with the cut command, we can use the pipe (|). This statement has the function of getting the output of the last command and sending it to the next command in the pipeline.

Example:

```
alisson@devops:~$ head -n3 /etc/passwd | cut -f 1,6,7 -d :
root:/root:/bin/bash
daemon:/usr/sbin:/usr/sbin/nologin
bin:/bin:/usr/sbin/nologin
```

Therefore, every time that you want to concatenate the commands, you must use the pipe (|). One interesting point is the second columns of the /etc/passwd file. I wrote that it is the password, but we can only see an x, this character represents the encrypted password. The hash can be found in the file /etc/shadow:

```
alisson@devops:~$ sudo head -n3 /etc/shadow
[sudo] password for alisson:
root:*:18113:0:99999:7:::
daemon:*:18113:0:99999:7:::
bin:*:18113:0:99999:7:::
```

To see the content of this file, you need to run the command sudo before the command head. The sudo command means the substitute users do. In a simple way, we are running the command head as we were another user. If you do not specify the user, by default, the user is root. The password is the same as we set in the installation. If you set the same password as me, it's devops.

To see your user's password, we can use the command `grep`. This command will find the line which corresponds with our criteria of the search.

Example:

`alisson@devops:~$ sudo grep alisson /etc/shadow`

`alisson:$6$aeR.OxEqoVMnyUuq$eYxtbG6V.156mtlsK9QBZcVOjQZBm7NlcKFn5x1y`
`xF4mffuLYd6Wmz2R9V2iKZvuC7fgp96H7.jlQW/o7OenF/:18292:0:99999:7:::`

Now you can clearly see the password hash in the second column. Of course, we cannot decrypt it, but if you want to take a Linux certification, you will need to record this file and the structures. However, we can also remove a user's password. You can just edit this file and delete the hash. This way, the user will not have a password and he can set a new one in the future.

Regarding the users, we also have one file on Linux to manage the groups. This file is located in /etc/group:

`alisson@devops:~$ head -n 3 /etc/group`

`root:x:0:`

`daemon:x:1:`

`bin:x:2:`

This file follows the following sequence:

`Group name | password | group id | users`

So, the users added into a group will appear in the last column of each line. As I explained earlier, we can use the command `grep` to find a group and see which users were added into it:

`alisson@devops:~$ grep sudo /etc/group`

`sudo:x:27:alisson`

It shows us one interesting thing; the command `sudo` only allows the users who belong to the `sudo` group to use the command. Another important file is the /etc/ fstab. This file is responsible to mount our volumes during the boot. Let's give it a look:

`alisson@devops:~$ cat /etc/fstab`

`UUID=75fbe5e6-26ff-4522-abc4-0d8a3ac69c5b / ext4 defaults 0 0`

`/swap.img        none      swap      sw       0        0`

When you work with Linux, it is really important for you to know the structure of the files. So, this file is organized in the following sequence:

`Partition - folder - filesystem type - mounting options - backup enable - disk check sequence`

Nowadays, this command lets you see the first column with a `uuid,` which represents a partition. If you want to see where it binds, run the following command:

alisson@devops:~$ **blkid**

/dev/sda2: UUID="75fbe5e6-26ff-4522-abc4-0d8a3ac69c5b" TYPE="ext4"
PARTUUID="7177f53d-2db2-49cb-93a9-21d763cac088"

If you check, it is exactly the same in the /etc/fstab. If you want to change, you can just replace the `uuid` in the file to /dev/sda2. It will work in the same way. The machine's hostname is stored in the /etc/hostname:

alisson@devops:~$ **cat /etc/hostname**

devops

If you want to change the hostname, you can just edit this file. We also have the /etc/hosts file that you can map an IP address to a name, as we did in the DNS:

alisson@devops:~$ **cat /etc/hosts**

127.0.0.1 localhost

127.0.1.1 devops

The following lines are desirable for IPv6 capable hosts

::1   ip6-localhost ip6-loopback

fe00::0 ip6-localnet

ff00::0 ip6-mcastprefix

ff02::1 ip6-allnodes

ff02::2 ip6-allrouters

It is very useful when you are developing a web system and you don't want to type the IP address in the browser every time a really important file is /etc/sudores:

alisson@devops:~$ **sudo cat /etc/sudoers**

[sudo] password for alisson:

#

This file MUST be edited with the 'visudo' command as root.

#

Please consider adding local content in /etc/sudoers.d/ instead of

directly modifying this file.

#

See the man page for details on how to write a sudoers file.

#

```
Defaults        env_reset
Defaults        mail_badpass
Defaults        secure_path="/usr/local/sbin:/usr/local/bin:/usr/sbin:/
usr/bin:/sbin:/bin:/snap/bin"

# Host alias specification

# User alias specification

# Cmnd alias specification

# User privilege specification
root    ALL=(ALL:ALL) ALL

# Members of the admin group may gain root privileges
%admin ALL=(ALL) ALL

# Allow members of group sudo to execute any command
%sudo   ALL=(ALL:ALL) ALL

# See sudoers(5) for more information on "#include" directives:

#includedir /etc/sudoers.d
```

This file is responsible to manage who can use the sudo command. I explained earlier, the only users in the group sudo can run the command. But, how does the command know which group it needs to use? Because of the following line:

```
# Allow members of group sudo to execute any command
%sudo   ALL=(ALL:ALL) ALL
```

You can put more groups in this file or you can put the users directly, like the following line:

```
# User privilege specification
root    ALL=(ALL:ALL) ALL
```

One thing that is nice to work with Linux is since all the documentation comes inside the files, like we saw in the /etc/sudoers, the comments explain how and where you have to edit the file. We also have the command man for that:

```
alisson@devops:~$ man sudo
```

```
SUDO(8)
BSD System Manager's Manual
```

```
SUDO(8)

NAME
    sudo, sudoedit — execute a command as another user
SYNOPSIS
    sudo -h | -K | -k | -V

    sudo -v [-AknS] [-a type] [-g group] [-h host] [-p prompt] [-u user]

    sudo -l [-AknS] [-a type] [-g group] [-h host] [-p prompt] [-U user]
[-u user] [command]

    sudo [-AbEHnPS] [-a type] [-C num] [-c class] [-g group] [-h host]
[-p prompt] [-r role] [-t type] [-T timeout] [-u user] [VAR=value] [-i |
-s] [command]

    sudoedit [-AknS] [-a type] [-C num] [-c class] [-g group] [-h host]
[-p prompt] [-T timeout] [-u user] file ...
```

This is just the first few lines of the file. To quit the man, press q. The file /etc/
crontab:

```
alisson@devops:~$ cat /etc/crontab

# /etc/crontab: system-wide crontab

# Unlike any other crontab you don't have to run the 'crontab'

# command to install the new version when you edit this file

# and files in /etc/cron.d. These files also have username fields,

# that none of the other crontabs do.

SHELL=/bin/sh

PATH=/usr/local/sbin:/usr/local/bin:/sbin:/bin:/usr/sbin:/usr/bin

# m h dom mon dow user   command

17 *    * * *    root    cd / && run-parts --report /etc/cron.hourly

25 6    * * *    root    test -x /usr/sbin/anacron || ( cd / && run-parts
--report /etc/cron.daily )

47 6    * * 7    root    test -x /usr/sbin/anacron || ( cd / && run-parts
--report /etc/cron.weekly )

52 6    1 * *    root    test -x /usr/sbin/anacron || ( cd / && run-parts
--report /etc/cron.monthly )

#
```

This is responsible to manage the scheduled tasks. It follows the following structure:

```
Minute - hour - day of the month - month - day of the week - user - command
```

So, if you want to schedule the tasks to run every `Friday` at `07` pm, you can add a line like the following:

```
00 19    * * 5    root    bash /bin/backup.sh
```

Therefore, every `Friday` at `7 pm`, the user root will run the command `backup.sh`. This is how we must read a line in the `crontab` file. This is the main file, but each user has their own `crontabs`, and they can be found in the following path:

```
alisson@devops:~$ sudo ls /var/spool/cron/crontabs/ -la
[sudo] password for alisson:
total 8
drwx-wx--T 2 root crontab 4096 Nov 16  2017 .
drwxr-xr-x 5 root root     4096 Aug  5  2019 ..
```

We do not have any file inside this directory, because we never created any schedule. But, we can edit the users' `crontab` for you to see the creation of the file. Type the following command in your terminal:

```
alisson@devops:~$ crontab -e
no crontab for alisson - using an empty one

Select an editor.  To change later, run 'select-editor'.
1. /bin/nano         <---- easiest
2. /usr/bin/vim.basic
3. /usr/bin/vim.tiny
4. /bin/ed

Choose 1-4 [1]: 2
crontab: installing new crontab
```

You can choose option 2, as I did. It will set the VIM as the default text editor for your `crontab`. Wait for the VIM to open and close by pressing *Esc,* and use the following command:

```
:wq!
```

I will explain more about VIM in the next section. Now that you have saved your user `crontab`, you can check the folder again:

```
alisson@devops:~$ sudo ls /var/spool/cron/crontabs/ -la
total 12
```

```
drwx-wx--T 2 root      crontab 4096 Feb 17 20:54 .
drwxr-xr-x 5 root      root    4096 Aug  5  2019 ..
-rw------- 1 alisson crontab 1089 Feb 17 20:54 alisson
```

You can see that a file with the same user's name was created. So, every user will have a file in this folder since they created a `crontab` using the command `crontab -e`. For Linux systems, it is a requirement to have an SSH connection and the configuration file for this is: `/etc/ssh/sshd_config`:

```
alisson@devops:~$ cat /etc/ssh/sshd_config
#         $OpenBSD: sshd_config,v 1.101 2017/03/14 07:19:07 djm Exp $

# This is the sshd server system-wide configuration file.  See
# sshd_config(5) for more information.

# This sshd was compiled with PATH=/usr/bin:/bin:/usr/sbin:/sbin

# The strategy used for options in the default sshd_config shipped with
# OpenSSH is to specify options with their default value where
# possible, but leave them commented.  Uncommented options override the
# default value.

#Port 22
#AddressFamily any
#ListenAddress 0.0.0.0
#ListenAddress ::
```

Formerly, we have a short part of the file, in which you are able to change the port, and define which IP addresses will listen for the connections:

```
alisson@devops:~$ grep Root /etc/ssh/sshd_config
#PermitRootLogin prohibit-password
# the setting of "PermitRootLogin without-password".
```

One important configuration in the preceding file, `PermitRootLogin`, is in some cases, we are able to login in the server using the root user directly. But, it is not a good practice. However, it is not uncommon to see in an on-premises environment. In the cloud environment, it is never allowed, because everyone in the world can try to access with the root user.

Another important configuration is the following one:

```
alisson@devops:~$ grep PasswordAuthentication /etc/ssh/sshd_config
```

```
#PasswordAuthentication yes

# PasswordAuthentication.  Depending on your PAM configuration,

# PAM authentication, then enable this but set PasswordAuthentication

PasswordAuthentication yes
```

If you are working with any Cloud provider like Amazon, Azure, or GCP, this configuration is disabled by default, for security reasons. We have added our SSH key in the server in the first chapter. So, if you want, you can edit this file and change the option for no.

Managing users and groups

Now, you already know some of the important files, and the files responsible to manage users and groups. We could just open these files and edit them to create new users and groups. But, Linux has useful commands which should be used to do that job and make our life easier.

Managing users

To see the users, we have the command getent:

```
alisson@devops:~$ getent passwd

root:x:0:0:root:/root:/bin/bash

daemon:x:1:1:daemon:/usr/sbin:/usr/sbin/nologin

bin:x:2:2:bin:/bin:/usr/sbin/nologin

sys:x:3:3:sys:/dev:/usr/sbin/nologin
```

The output is a quite similar as the command cat, but, the difference is that we can look for a specific user, like we did using the command grep:

```
alisson@devops:~$ getent passwd alisson

alisson:x:1000:1000:alisson:/home/alisson:/bin/bash
```

Thus, it is up to you which command you want to use. When I am working, I always use the getent, to look for a user or group, and the grep command, to find a line in any file of the Linux system.

To add a new user, run the following command:

```
alisson@devops:~$ sudo adduser elvis

[sudo] password for alisson:

Adding user 'elvis' ...

Adding new group 'elvis' (1001) ...

Adding new user 'elvis' (1001) with group 'elvis' ...
```

```
Creating home directory '/home/elvis' ...
Copying files from '/etc/skel' ...
Enter new UNIX password:
Retype new UNIX password:
passwd: password updated successfully
Changing the user information for elvis
Enter the new value, or press ENTER for the default
    Full Name []:
    Room Number []:
    Work Phone []:
    Home Phone []:
    Other []:
Is the information correct? [Y/n]
```

Only the username and password are mandatory. You can leave the other options blank, as I did in the example. I set the password as **devops**. If you analyze the command output, you can see two things that are important for us to pay attention.

The first is the information about the **home** directory. The command creates a folder called **elvis** within the /home folder. As I explained earlier, the **home** folder is responsible for the user's files.

The second is the /etc/skel, where the command **adduser** gets the default files present in the **home** folder of the user. We can give it a look with the following command:

```
alisson@devops:~$ ls /etc/skel/ -la
total 20
drwxr-xr-x  2 root root 4096 Aug  5  2019 .
drwxr-xr-x 91 root root 4096 Feb 18 19:25 ..
-rw-r--r--  1 root root  220 Apr  4  2018 .bash_logout
-rw-r--r--  1 root root 3771 Apr  4  2018 .bashrc
-rw-r--r--  1 root root  807 Apr  4  2018 .profile
```

These files are responsible to customize the user's environment. We are going to edit them in the last part of this chapter. But, if you want to put more items inside the home folder, you can just add inside the /etc/skel, and they will be present for the next user created. Let's test it.

Let's create a skeleton for a hosting server. How does the web server work? Usually, we have the user and in the **home** folder of each user, you have some folder called, `public_html`, `mail`, `conf`, `logs`. All these folders must be created at the same time as the user is created. So, run the following command:

```
alisson@devops:~$ sudo mkdir /etc/skel/{public_html, logs, mail, conf}
[sudo] password for alisson:
alisson@devops:~$ ls /etc/skel/
conf  logs  mail  public_html
alisson@devops:~$
```

So, as you can see, now we have these four folders created inside the /etc/skel. Now, let's create another user to see it working:

```
alisson@devops:~$ sudo adduser customer01
Adding user 'customer01' ...
Adding new group 'customer01' (1002) ...
Adding new user 'customer01' (1002) with group 'customer01' ...
Creating home directory '/home/customer01' ...
Copying files from '/etc/skel' ...
Enter new UNIX password:
Retype new UNIX password:
passwd: password updated successfully
Changing the user information for customer01
Enter the new value, or press ENTER for the default
    Full Name []:
    Room Number []:
    Work Phone []:
    Home Phone []:
    Other []:
Is the information correct? [Y/n]
alisson@devops:~$ ls /home/customer01/
conf  logs  mail  public_html
```

As you can see now, we have these folders created in the home folder of the user. I am setting the same password for all users. But, if you forgot a password and you want to change it, the command to do that is as follows:

```
alisson@devops:~$ sudo passwd elvis
Enter new UNIX password:
Retype new UNIX password:
```

```
passwd: password updated successfully
```

Now, type the new password and it is changed.

We are now talking about the hosting servers. So, let's use another example. Imagine your customer did not pay you. So, you need to block this user. To execute this task, you can run the following command:

```
alisson@devops:~$ sudo passwd -l customer01
```

```
passwd: password expiry information changed.
```

One interesting thing about Linux is if you want to know how it blocks the users, you can give a look at the /etc/shadow:

```
alisson@devops:~$ sudo getent shadow customer01
```

```
customer01:!$6$PExBAe3N$6AxVOOJLi/A5ddWOp2I/ZhvB00mpVwq4KQ78/4.
QNNcrz2tsGGFu8XXr/TU7NFA/Hg3T2X9.R5v6cCuzbYF8j.:18310:0:99999:7:::
```

Paying attention to the output is easy. To note one difference, let's compare with a non-blocked user:

```
alisson@devops:~$ sudo getent shadow alisson
```

```
alisson:$6$aeR.OxEqoVMnyUuq$eYxtbG6V.156mtlsK9QBZcVOjQZBm7NlcKFn5x1
yxF4mffuLYd6Wmz2R9V2iKZvuC7fgp96H7.jlQW/o7OenF/:18292:0:99999:7:::
```

In the second column, where the password is stored, for a blocked user, you can see that the system puts an exclamation point (!) as the first character. This way, the user can type his password and it will never match with the hash because there is an exclamation point in the beginning.

To unblock the user, type the following command:

```
alisson@devops:~$ sudo passwd -u customer01
```

```
passwd: password expiry information changed.
```

```
alisson@devops:~$ sudo getent shadow customer01
```

```
customer01:$6$PExBAe3N$6AxVOOJLi/A5ddWOp2I/ZhvB00mpVwq4KQ78/4.
QNNcrz2tsGGFu8XXr/TU7NFA/Hg3T2X9.R5v6cCuzbYF8j.:18310:0:99999:7:::
```

Now, Linux removed the ! in the beginning of the hash and the user is able to access the shell again. If the customer canceled the service with you, it is possible to remove his user. To execute this task, you need to run the following command:

```
alisson@devops:~$ sudo userdel elvis
```

```
alisson@devops:~$ sudo getent passwd elvis
```

It is important to remember that removing the user does not mean you will remove his home directory if we check:

```
alisson@devops:~$ ls /home/
```

alisson   customer01   elvis

You can remove it manually now using the following command.

alisson@devops:~$ **sudo rm -rf /home/elvis/**

Linux has this behavior to avoid you delete files that you might need in the future. But, if you are sure you want to remove everything, run the following command:

alisson@devops:~$ **sudo userdel -r customer01**

userdel: customer01 mail spool (/var/mail/customer01) not found

alisson@devops:~$ **ls /home/**

alisson

Now, everything is deleted.

Managing groups

This task is pretty similar to the user management. We can see all the groups:

alisson@devops:~$ **sudo getent group**

root:x:0:

daemon:x:1:

bin:x:2:

sys:x:3:

adm:x:4:syslog,Alisson

Find a group using a specific name:

alisson@devops:~$ **sudo getent group sudo**

sudo:x:27:Alisson

Create a new user and add this user to the group sudo:

alisson@devops:~$ **sudo useradd gabriela**

alisson@devops:~$ **sudo getent passwd gabriela**

gabriela:x:1001:1001::/home/gabriela:/bin/sh

alisson@devops:~$ **sudo getent group sudo**

sudo:x:27:Alisson

The command I ran showed that I created a user called gabriela. This user is present in the passwd file and the group sudo just had the user Alisson added. To add the new user, run the following command:

alisson@devops:~$ **sudo gpasswd -a gabriela sudo**

Adding user gabriela to group sudo

```
alisson@devops:~$ sudo getent group sudo
```

```
sudo:x:27:alisson,gabriela
```

Perfect! Now, we have 2 users who belong the sudo group and we can switch the user to see if the new one has the same permissions:

```
alisson@devops:~$ sudo su - gabriela
```

```
No directory, logging in with HOME=/
```

```
$
```

One interesting point is if you paid attention, I ran 2 different commands to create a user .Firstly, I ran the adduser and after I ran useradd. What is the difference between the commands?

The last output when I changed the user using the command su -, I received the message of no directory for this user. Therefore, the command useradd does not create the home folder for the user as the adduser does. So, we can use the useradd for the technical user, which does not need a password or home directory, and the adduser for common users. Do I use that in my daily work? No, I use the adduser for everything and after that, I remove the shell and the password, like the following:

```
alisson@devops:~$ sudo adduser app1 --shell /bin/false

Adding user 'app1' ...

Adding new group 'app1' (1002) ...

Adding new user 'app1' (1002) with group 'app1' ...

Creating home directory '/home/app1' ...

Copying files from '/etc/skel' ...

Enter new UNIX password:

Retype new UNIX password:

passwd: password updated successfully

Changing the user information for app1

Enter the new value, or press ENTER for the default

    Full Name []:

    Room Number []:

    Work Phone []:

    Home Phone []:

    Other []:

Is the information correct? [Y/n]

alisson@devops:~$ sudo passwd -l app1
```

```
passwd: password expiry information changed.
alisson@devops:~$ sudo getent shadow app1
app1:!$6$Arm1hXou$Ry11spiafwXfqcPkVQ3xJDCd4gbN9vcsw1.9wkDoO4N69.
3vnkHTZl.jPsMJLJmYjJwW4yS.CvvMEA5bGsZVE1:18312:0:99999:7:::

alisson@devops:~$ sudo getent passwd app1
app1:x:1002:1002:,,,:/home/app1:/bin/false
```

So, if you check the output, you can clearly see that the user has no shell and he is blocked for login. It would be so much easier if I had executed the useradd. But, when you develop a vicious circle, it is hard to avoid.

Now, let's get back to the users in the group sudo. Deleting the user:

```
alisson@devops:~$ sudo userdel -r gabriela
userdel: gabriela mail spool (/var/mail/gabriela) not found
userdel: gabriela home directory (/home/gabriela) not found
```

Creating the user again:

```
alisson@devops:~$ sudo adduser gabriela
Adding user 'gabriela' ...
Adding new group 'gabriela' (1001) ...
Adding new user 'gabriela' (1001) with group 'gabriela' ...
Creating home directory '/home/gabriela' ...
Copying files from '/etc/skel' ...
Enter new UNIX password:
Retype new UNIX password:
passwd: password updated successfully
Changing the user information for gabriela
Enter the new value, or press ENTER for the default
    Full Name []:
    Room Number []:
    Work Phone []:
    Home Phone []:
    Other []:
Is the information correct? [Y/n]
```

Adding the user to the group:

```
alisson@devops:~$ sudo gpasswd -a  gabriela  sudo
Adding user gabriela to group sudo
alisson@devops:~$
```

Changing the user:

```
alisson@devops:~$ sudo su - gabriela
To run a command as administrator (user "root"), use "sudo <command>".
See "man sudo_root" for details.

gabriela@devops:~$
```

Now, you are able to see that my shell has changed. Now, I am the user `gabriela`. To create users or groups, we need to have the `sudo` permission. Let's try to create a new group called `applications`:

```
gabriela@devops:~$ sudo addgroup applications
[sudo] password for gabriela:
Adding group 'applications' (GID 1003) ...
Done.
```

Checking if the group was created:

```
gabriela@devops:~$ sudo getent group applications
applications:x:1003:
```

Adding a new user to this group:

```
gabriela@devops:~$ sudo useradd juergen

gabriela@devops:~$ sudo gpasswd -a juergen applications
#Adding user juergen to group applications:
gabriela@devops:~$ getent group applications
applications:x:1003:juergen
```

And if you want to delete the group:

```
gabriela@devops:~$ sudo delgroup applications
Removing group 'applications' ...
Done.
```

Switching back to my user:

```
gabriela@devops:~$ exit
```

```
logout
alisson@devops:~$
```

And that is it. This was your **QuickStart** for managing user and groups. Of course, we could go so much deeper in these topics, but I still have to explain how you can customize your environment.

Working with Permissions

The Linux permission system works differently from Windows. We have some numbers associated with the permission. So, for example:

1 – Execution

2 - Writing

4 – Reading

So you always have to make some math to apply for the permission. If you want to assign the execution permission you can set as **1**, write permission **2** and reading permission **4**. `Write` + `Reading` is equal to 6, so the permission is 6. If you want `Read` `+ Write + Execution` is equal to 7. Let's create a file and check its permissions:

```
alisson@devops:~$ touch new_file

alisson@devops:~$ ls -la new_file

-rw-rw-r-- 1 alisson alisson 0 Feb 20 19:21 new_file
```

The command touch is responsible to change the access time of any file. If the file does not exist, it creates one. Checking the output, you can see that we have the permissions: read+write, read+write, read, but what means that sequence:

```
user - group - other
```

In the same line, we can see `alisson alisson`, the first one is the user owner for this file and the second one is the group. By default, all the users created on Linux have a group with the same name as the user.

If you remember the numbers which represent the permission, we can make a calculation, `read+write = 4 + 2 = 6`. Then we have the following permissions:

```
664
```

Therefore, the user can read and write. Users from the same group can also read and write, users who do not belong to the group can just read. Now, we can create a directory and analyze the permissions as we did just now:

```
alisson@devops:~$ mkdir new_folder

alisson@devops:~$ ls -la  | grep new_folder

drwxrwxr-x 2 alisson alisson 4096 Feb 20 19:29 new_folder
```

Analyzing the permissions, we can see, `read + write + execution` for the user and group, and `read + execution` for the others. If we make the following association:

```
read + write + execution = 4 + 2 + 1 = 7
read + execution = 4 + 1 = 5
```

Then, we have 775. What can we conclude, then? The default permissions for the files are 644, and for the directories are 775.

> **Why are the permissions for the directories and the files different? If we paid attention, the only difference is Execution. The files are created without this, just for security. So, we can execute the wrong files, and the folders are created with the execution permission because with this permission, we can open the folders.**

Nice, but how can we change the file permissions?

Changing read and write permissions

The command used for changing these permissions is `chmod`. I will show you how we can change it using numbers and letters. The experienced Linux users usually use numbers, but it does not make any difference whether you use numbers or letters. Let's use an example of the new_file:

```
alisson@devops:~$ ls -la new_file
-rw-rw-r-- 1 alisson alisson 0 Feb 20 19:21 new_file
```

So, the permission is 664, which means that any user who is not me can read the file content and I do not want to allow it. So, I will change the permission for other users to 0:

```
alisson@devops:~$ chmod 660 new_file
alisson@devops:~$ ls -la new_file
-rw-rw---- 1 alisson alisson 0 Feb 20 19:21 new_file
```

I just changed the permissions for 660. So, let's create the content inside this file. Change the user and see how it works:

```
alisson@devops:~$ echo content not allowed to other > new_file
alisson@devops:~$ cat new_file
content not allowed to other
```

Let's change the user to gabriela:

```
alisson@devops:~$ sudo su - gabriela
[sudo] password for alisson:

gabriela@devops:~$ pwd
/home/gabriela
```

```
gabriela@devops:~$ ls -la /home
total 20
drwxr-xr-x  5 root     root     4096 Feb 20 19:05 .
drwxr-xr-x 24 root     root     4096 Feb 18 18:00 ..
drwxr-xr-x  6 alisson  alisson  4096 Feb 20 19:29 alisson
drwxr-xr-x  6 app1     app1     4096 Feb 20 19:00 app1
drwxr-xr-x  6 gabriela gabriela 4096 Feb 20 19:12 gabriela
```

Now, I will enter in my home folder and try to see the file content:

```
gabriela@devops:~$ cd /home/alisson/
```

```
gabriela@devops:/home/alisson$ cat new_file
cat: new_file: Permission denied
```

And it works! But, if we remember the managing groups' part, this user has permission to use sudo. So, I will add itself in the group Alisson, and let's see what happens:

```
gabriela@devops:/home/alisson$ sudo gpasswd -a gabriela alisson
[sudo] password for gabriela:
Adding user gabriela to group Alisson
```

If we type the command groups, we can see the groups that this user belongs to:

```
gabriela@devops:/home/alisson$ groups
gabriela sudo
```

Thus, it means that the new user is not able to be used in this session. Let's logout and login again, and see if it changes:

```
gabriela@devops:/home/alisson$ logout
alisson@devops:~$ sudo su - gabriela
gabriela@devops:~$ groups
gabriela sudo alisson
```

Now, the group is loaded. So, let's try to see the file content again:

```
gabriela@devops:~$ cd /home/alisson/
```

```
gabriela@devops:/home/alisson$ cat new_file
content not allowed to other
```

And it is possible to see the file content. So this is how the permission works. I show how we can change the permission using the number. If you want to change it using letters, it is basically the same. Let's try:

```
gabriela@devops:/home/alisson$ cd
```

```
gabriela@devops:~$ touch letters_file
gabriela@devops:~$ ls -la letters_file
-rw-rw-r-- 1 gabriela gabriela 0 Feb 20 19:47 letters_file
```

To remove all the permission to others:

```
gabriela@devops:~$ chmod o= letters_file
gabriela@devops:~$ ls -la letters_file
-rw-rw---- 1 gabriela gabriela 0 Feb 20 19:47 letters_file
```

Then, we can see that I just had to type o=, which means other = nothing, and the permissions were set. I could just add the execution permission:

```
gabriela@devops:~$ chmod o+x letters_file
gabriela@devops:~$ ls -la letters_file
-rw-rw---x 1 gabriela gabriela 0 Feb 20 19:47 letters_file
```

Or, I can set the permissions to read for all, and write just for the owner:

```
gabriela@devops:~$ chmod g=rx,o=rx letters_file
gabriela@devops:~$ ls -la letters_file
-rw-r-xr-x 1 gabriela gabriela 0 Feb 20 19:47 letters_file
```

And if I want to give the write permission to everyone, I will do the following:

```
gabriela@devops:~$ chmod +w letters_file
gabriela@devops:~$ ls -la letters_file
-rw-rwxr-x 1 gabriela gabriela 0 Feb 20 19:47 letters_file
```

The same command works for the directories.

Change the owner of files and executing scripts

The same way as chmod is used for permissions, chown is used for ownership. Let me use the same files that we have:

```
gabriela@devops:~$ ls -la letters_file
-rw-rwxr-x 1 gabriela gabriela 0 Feb 20 19:47 letters_file
```

The owner is gabriela, and the group is gabriela too. In the previous example, I have added the user gabriela to the group alisson, and then the user was able to access the file. But this time, I will do it differently:

```
gabriela@devops:~$ chown gabriela:alisson letters_file
gabriela@devops:~$ ls -la letters_file
-rw-rwxr-x 1 gabriela alisson 0 Feb 20 19:47 letters_file
```

Now, the group owner for this file is alisson. If I want to change the user, I can run the command as follows:

```
gabriela@devops:~$ sudo chown juergen letters_file
[sudo] password for gabriela:

gabriela@devops:~$ ls -la letters_file
-rw-rwxr-x 1 juergen alisson 0 Feb 20 19:47 letters_file
```

Jurgen is the owner of this file. We can use the command chown to change the user and the group for a file or directory. But we have a command which can also be used to change the group:

```
gabriela@devops:~$ sudo chgrp gabriela letters_file

gabriela@devops:~$ ls -la letters_file

-rw-rwxr-x 1 juergen gabriela 0 Feb 20 19:47 letters_file
```

The group is now changed. Therefore, the command chgrp changes only the group, and the command chown changes the owner, or the owner and the group. Thus, to finish this chapter, we are just missing to see how to execute a script. So let's create a simple one:

```
gabriela@devops:~$ echo "echo this is a simple script"> simple_script.sh

gabriela@devops:~$ ls -la simple_script.sh

-rw-rw-r-- 1 gabriela gabriela 29 Feb 20 20:05 simple_script.sh
```

Here, we have the script created. To execute it, run it as follows:

```
gabriela@devops:~$ ./simple_script.sh

-su: ./simple_script.sh: Permission denied
```

Permission denied! This happens because, if we analyze the previous command run and check the permissions, there is no x, which represents the execution permission. Then, set the following permission:

```
gabriela@devops:~$ chmod +x simple_script.sh
```

Run the script again:

```
gabriela@devops:~$ ./simple_script.sh

this is a simple script
```

Let's check the permissions one more time:

```
gabriela@devops:~$ ls -la simple_script.sh

-rwxrwxr-x 1 gabriela gabriela 29 Feb 20 20:05 simple_script.sh
```

The x is in all the permission groups for the users, groups, and others. So, everyone can execute it. If you still give the execution just for the file owner or for the group, you can use chmod for it, and use the same math to set the permissions.

CHAPTER 3
Setting Up a Service

This chapter will explain how the Linux Package system works, how to install a package, install a service, configure it, and run your first application in your first LAMP (Linux Apache MySQL PHP) server.

Structure

In this chapter, we will discuss the following topics:

- Learning how to install a package
  - APT
- Installing the Apache
  - Configuring your service
  - Creating a VHost
- Installing MySQL
  - Configuring the service
  - Creating a database and tables
- Deploying your application
  - Installing PHP
  - Deploying WordPress

Objectives

After studying this unit, you should be able to:

- Understand the Linux package system
- Install packages using APT
- Setup a web server
- Setup a database server
- Deploy an application

Learning how to install a package

Most of the Linux distributions have a package manager by default. It can be YUM, APT, Zypper, pacman, slackapt, etc. Each one has its own particularities, but all were made for the same purpose, to install the packages that are basically the Linux programs, via centralized repositories which are distributed all over the world.

In the first chapter, I gave a brief explanation about the Linux distributions and some differences. Some of them are in the package management systems. Now, I am going to give 2 examples of the most famous package managers.

Debian based distributions, like Ubuntu, have the **APT** (**Advanced Package Tool**). It connects to a central repository like this: **http://de.archive.ubuntu.com/ubuntu**. It is just an Apache web server, and in it, are stored several packages which we can choose and install.

RedHat based distributions, like CentOS, have **YUM** (**Yellow Dog Update Manager**), which will soon be replaced by the **DNF** (**Dandified Yum**), the new substitute of YUM. It also uses a central repository like **https://dl.fedoraproject.org/pub/epel/7/x86_64/,** and also stores several packages.

Now, let's focus on Debian which is our goal here, once we are using Ubuntu.

APT

If you run just the command `apt` without any parameter, you will see the following output:

```
alisson@devops:~$ apt
apt 1.6.11 (amd64)
Usage: apt [options] command

apt is a commandline package manager and provides commands for
searching and managing as well as querying information about packages.
```

It provides the same functionality as the specialized APT tools, like apt-get and apt-cache, but enables options more suitable for interactive use by default.

Most used commands:
    list - list packages based on package names
    search - search in package descriptions
    show - show package details
    install - install packages
    remove - remove packages
    autoremove - Remove automatically all unused packages
    update - update list of available packages
    upgrade - upgrade the system by installing/upgrading packages
    full-upgrade - upgrade the system by removing/installing/upgrading packages
    edit-sources - edit the source information file

See apt(8) for more information about the available commands.

Configuration options and syntax is detailed in apt.conf(5).

Information about how to configure sources can be found in sources. list(5).

Package and version choices can be expressed via apt_preferences(5).

Security details are available in apt-secure(8).

This APT has Super Cow Powers.

Therefore, the options are self-explained. Let's use them in practice. One interesting thing is the command top:

top - 18:19:11 up 2 days, 2:34, 1 user, load average: 0.04, 0.03, 0.00

Tasks: 92 total,   1 running, 50 sleeping,   0 stopped,   0 zombie

%Cpu(s): 0.0 us, 0.0 sy, 0.0 ni,100.0 id, 0.0 wa, 0.0 hi, 0.0 si, 0.0 st

KiB Mem : 1008816 total,   133020 free,   126512 used,   749284 buff/ cache

KiB Swap: 2017276 total, 2016752 free,   524 used.   716548 avail Mem

PID	USER	PR	NI	VIRT	RES	SHR	S	%CPU	%MEM	TIME+	COMMAND
28427	alisson	20	0	107988	3460	2448	S	0.3	0.3	0:00.14	sshd

```
28462 alisson    20   0   42788    3940    3344 R  0.3  0.4   0:00.25 top
    1 root       20   0   77992    9104    6680 S  0.0  0.9   0:02.58 systemd
    2 root       20   0       0       0       0 S  0.0  0.0   0:00.00 kthreadd
    4 root        0 -20       0       0       0 I  0.0  0.0   0:00.00 kworker/0:0H
    6 root        0 -20       0       0       0 I  0.0  0.0   0:00.00 mm_
percpu_wq
    7 root       20   0       0       0       0 S  0.0  0.0   0:00.55 ksoftirqd/0
    8 root       20   0       0       0       0 I  0.0  0.0   0:19.94 rcu_sched
```

To exit from the top, press q. This command basically shows the current state of your machine, the state of memory, CPU, processes running, etc. There is another version of top which is called **htop.** It does exactly the same thing. However, it has a better interface, and therefore, before we install that version, run the following command:

alisson@devops:~$ sudo su -

[sudo] password for alisson:

root@devops:~#

The previous command changes your current user to the user root. Until now, we were running the command sudo before every command which needs more permission. Now, we need not type sudo before the command every time because we are already the administrator of this server. Or, you can say that we are the root user.

Sometimes, when we create a server based on an image. The local cache of APT is completely outdated. So, we need to clean it and update using the following commands:

root@devops:~# apt clean

root@devops:~# **apt update**

Hit:1 http://de.archive.ubuntu.com/ubuntu bionic InRelease

Hit:2 http://de.archive.ubuntu.com/ubuntu bionic-updates InRelease

Hit:3 http://de.archive.ubuntu.com/ubuntu bionic-backports InRelease

Hit:4 http://de.archive.ubuntu.com/ubuntu bionic-security InRelease

Reading package lists... Done

Building dependency tree

Reading state information... Done

65 packages can be upgraded. Run 'apt list --upgradable' to see them.

root@devops:~#

Now, you have the local cache updated. We can try to find the htop and see if it is available to install:

```
root@devops:~# apt search htop
Sorting... Done
Full Text Search... Done
aha/bionic 0.4.10.6-4 amd64
ANSI color to HTML converter

htop/bionic,now 2.1.0-3 amd64 [installed,automatic]
interactive processes viewer

libauthen-oath-perl/bionic 2.0.1-1 all
Perl module for OATH One Time Passwords

pftools/bionic 3+dfsg-2build1 amd64
build and search protein and DNA generalized profiles
```

Analyzing the previous output, we can say that htop is available. So, to install the package, we use the following command:

```
root@devops:~# apt install htop -y
Reading package lists... Done
Building dependency tree
Reading state information... Done
htop is already the newest version (2.1.0-3).
htop set to manually installed.
0 upgraded, 0 newly installed, 0 to remove and 65 not upgraded.
root@devops:~#
```

The package is installed now. So, run the following command:

```
CPU[
0.0%]    Tasks: 29, 28 thr; 1 running
Mem[|||||||||||||||||||||||||||||||||||||||||||||||||||||||||||||||||||||||||12
8M/985M]    Load average: 0.07 0.02 0.00
Swp[|
524K/1.92G]    Uptime: 2 days, 02:45:09

PID USER      PRI  NI  VIRT   RES    SHR S CPU% MEM%   TIME+  Command
28771 root      20   0 32468  4868   3764 R  0.0  0.5  0:00.02 htop
1 root        20   0 77992  9104   6680 S  0.0  0.9  0:02.58 /sbin/init
maybe-ubiquity

394 root        19  -1  100M 17652 16796 S  0.0  1.7  0:00.36 /lib/
```

```
systemd/systemd-journald
420 root         20   0  103M  1852  1664 S  0.0  0.2  0:00.00 /sbin/
lvmetad -f
421 root         20   0 45836  4476  2888 S  0.0  0.4  0:00.87 /lib/
systemd/systemd-udevd
496 systemd-t 20    0   138M  3256  2744 S  0.0  0.3  0:00.00 /lib/
systemd/systemd-timesyncd
491 systemd-t 20    0   138M  3256  2744 S  0.0  0.3  0:00.20 /lib/
systemd/systemd-timesyncd
672 systemd-n 20    0 80048  5076  4484 S  0.0  0.5  0:00.19 /lib/
systemd/systemd-networkd
696 systemd-r 20    0 70636  4916  4356 S  0.0  0.5  0:00.19 /lib/
systemd/systemd-resolved
```

In this simple output, we are able to see some improvements. For example, we now have a bar to indicate the amount of memory used in the server. It is a good tool to analyze the current state of your server, but, it is not used much in the production system because it consumes more memory than the traditional top. So, let's remove this package using the following command:

```
root@devops:~# apt remove htop
Reading package lists... Done
Building dependency tree
Reading state information... Done
The following packages will be REMOVED:
htop ubuntu-server
0 upgraded, 0 newly installed, 2 to remove and 64 not upgraded.
After this operation, 269 kB disk space will be freed.
Do you want to continue? [Y/n] y
(Reading database ... 102467 files and directories currently installed.)
Removing ubuntu-server (1.417.3) ...
Removing htop (2.1.0-3) ...
Processing triggers for mime-support (3.60ubuntu1) ...
Processing triggers for man-db (2.8.3-2ubuntu0.1) ...
```

These are all the commands you will probably use in your daily work while installing the packages on Linux. Beside the commands, we also have some important files which are required to install some packages that may not be available in the official repositories.

The first important file is `/etc/apt/sources.list`:

```
root@devops:~# cat /etc/apt/sources.list

# See http://help.ubuntu.com/community/UpgradeNotes for how to upgrade
to

# newer versions of the distribution.


deb http://de.archive.ubuntu.com/ubuntu bionic main restricted

deb http://de.archive.ubuntu.com/ubuntu bionic-updates main restricted
```

Above-mentioned is an example of the first few entries from the `sources.list`. These are the lines representing the remote repositories where the packages are found. If you want to add a new repository, you can just find the respective line and add at the end of this file, for example:

```
deb http://ppa.launchpad.net/canonical-kernel-team/unstable/ubuntu
bionic main
```

In the beginning of the URL, you can see that it starts with **PPA (Personal Packages Archines)**. These are the useful repositories that are not included in the distribution by default, but you may find some packages which you want to use.

Another important directory is: `/var/cache/apt/`. In the beginning, I explained that the APT stores the cache inside the Linux, and if it is too old, we need to clean and update it. This folder also downloads the packages installed in our system, for example:

```
root@devops:~# apt install htop --download-only

Reading package lists... Done

Building dependency tree

Reading state information... Done

The following NEW packages will be installed:

htop

0 upgraded, 1 newly installed, 0 to remove and 64 not upgraded.

Need to get 80.0 kB of archives.

After this operation, 221 kB of additional disk space will be used.

Get:1 http://de.archive.ubuntu.com/ubuntu bionic/main amd64 htop amd64
2.1.0-3 [80.0 kB]

Fetched 80.0 kB in 0s (451 kB/s)

Download complete and in download only mode
```

I ran the APT installation just to download the package using the option –download-only, and if we check the directory:

```
root@devops:~# ls /var/cache/apt/archives/
htop_2.1.0-3_amd64.deb  lock  partial
```

You can see the package there. Now, if you run the following clean command:

```
root@devops:~# apt clean
```

```
root@devops:~# ls /var/cache/apt/archives/
lock  partial
```

The package is not there anymore.

Installing Apache

We installed one basic package to learn how APT works. Now, let's install a real one. The Apache web server is currently the most used web servers in the world. You can deploy any application using it as a Load Balancer, cache for static files, proxy for another web server, and many other options that depend on your usage. To install Apache, use the following command:

```
root@devops:~# apt install apache2 -y

Reading package lists... Done

Building dependency tree

Reading state information... Done
```

The following additional packages will be installed:

```
apache2-bin apache2-data apache2-utils libapr1 libaprutil1 libaprutil1-
dbd-sqlite3 libaprutil1-ldap liblua5.2-0 ssl-cert
```

If the installation ran well for you, it is possible to validate if Apache is installed and running using the following command:

```
root@devops:~# service apache2 status

apache2.service - The Apache HTTP Server

Loaded: loaded (/lib/systemd/system/apache2.service; disabled; vendor
preset: enabled)

Drop-In: /lib/systemd/system/apache2.service.d
          └apache2-systemd.conf

Active: active (running) since Mon 2020-07-06 12:56:38 UTC; 11s ago

Process: 22810 ExecStart=/usr/sbin/apachectl start (code=exited,
status=0/SUCCESS)
```

Pay attention to the part where says it **Active** (running), or, you can also use the command ss -ntpl:

```
root@devops:~# ss -ntpl
```

```
State                       Recv-Q                    Send-Q
Local Address:Port                                    Peer Address:Port

LISTEN                      0                         128
127.0.0.53%lo:53                                              0.0.0.0:*
users:(("systemd-resolve",pid=694,fd=13))

LISTEN                      0                         128
0.0.0.0:22                                                    0.0.0.0:*
users:(("sshd",pid=1113,fd=3))

LISTEN                      0                         12
8                                                     *:80
*:*                                 users:(("apache2",pid=22842,fd=4),("apache2",pi
d=22841,fd=4),("apache2",pid= 22840,fd=4),("apache2",pid=22839,fd=4),(
"apache2",pid=22838,fd=4),("apache2",pid=22835,fd=4))

LISTEN                      0                         128
[::]:22                                                       [::]:*
users:(("sshd",pid=1113,fd=4))
```

We can see Apache running on port 80, with the PID 22848. PID means process identification. Now, the server is up and running. Let's check the access via browser:

`http://192.168.178.62/`

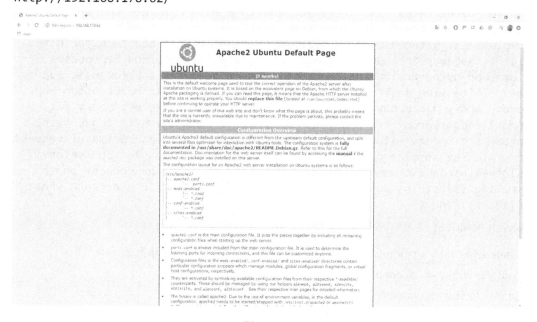

Figure 3.1

This is the Apache default page when the server is running on Ubuntu. Usually, this page is different depending on your OS.

Now, you can say that you have setup a web server. However, we know that the websites are not just made using HTML. There is a lot of back-end processing. Usually, it is PHP. Of course, you can develop your website using any of the dozens of programming languages that are available. But, I am still pretty sure that PHP is the most common used for most of the websites.

Installing PHP

In this part, let's install PHP and create a simple page to check if it is installed, and what are the modules available to use with it:

```
root@devops:~# apt install php -y
```

The installation is simple using APT. When we install PHP and Apache, there are many Apache modules that are installed together. You can run the following command to check them:

```
root@devops:~# a2enmod
```

```
Your choices are: access_compat actions alias allowmethods asis auth_
basic auth_digest auth_form authn_anon authn_core authn_dbd authn_dbm
authn_file authn_socache authnz_fcgi authnz_ldap authz_core authz_dbd
authz_dbm authz_groupfile authz_host authz_owner authz_user autoindex
buffer cache cache_disk cache_socache cern_meta cgi cgid charset_
lite data dav dav_fs dav_lock dbd deflate dialup dir dump_io echo env
expires ext_filter file_cache filter headers heartbeat heartmonitor http2
ident imagemap include info lbmethod_bybusyness lbmethod_byrequests
lbmethod_bytraffic lbmethod_heartbeat ldap log_debug log_forensic lua
macro mime mime_magic mpm_event mpm_preforkmpm_worker negotiation php7.2
proxy proxy_ajp proxy_balancer proxy_connectproxy_express proxy_fcgi
proxy_fdpass proxy_ftp proxy_hcheck proxy_html proxy_http proxy_http2
proxy_scgi proxy_wstunnel ratelimit reflector remoteip reqtimeout request
rewrite sed session session_cookie session_crypto session_dbd setenvif
slotmem_plain slotmem_shm socache_dbm socache_memcache socache_shmcb
speling ssl status substitute suexec unique_id userdir usertrack vhost_
alias xml2enc
```

```
Which module(s) do you want to enable (wildcards ok)?
```

There are many options, but the one we are looking for is php7.2:

```
root@devops:~# a2enmod php7.2
```

```
Considering dependency mpm_prefork for php7.2:
```

```
Considering conflict mpm_event for mpm_prefork:
```

```
Considering conflict mpm_worker for mpm_prefork:
```

```
Module mpm_prefork already enabled
```

```
Considering conflict php5 for php7.2:
```

```
Module php7.2 already enabled
```

The command `a2enmod`, enables the `php7.2` module, which is responsible to integrate Apache and PHP. When we access a PHP page via a browser, Apache will call that module which will call the PHP interpreter and run the code. Let's create a simple page as an example:

```
root@devops:~# vim /var/www/html/info.php

<?php

phpinfo();

?>
```

This code is the simplest code that you can run on PHP to check if everything is running. When you call that page via a browser, you will see the following:

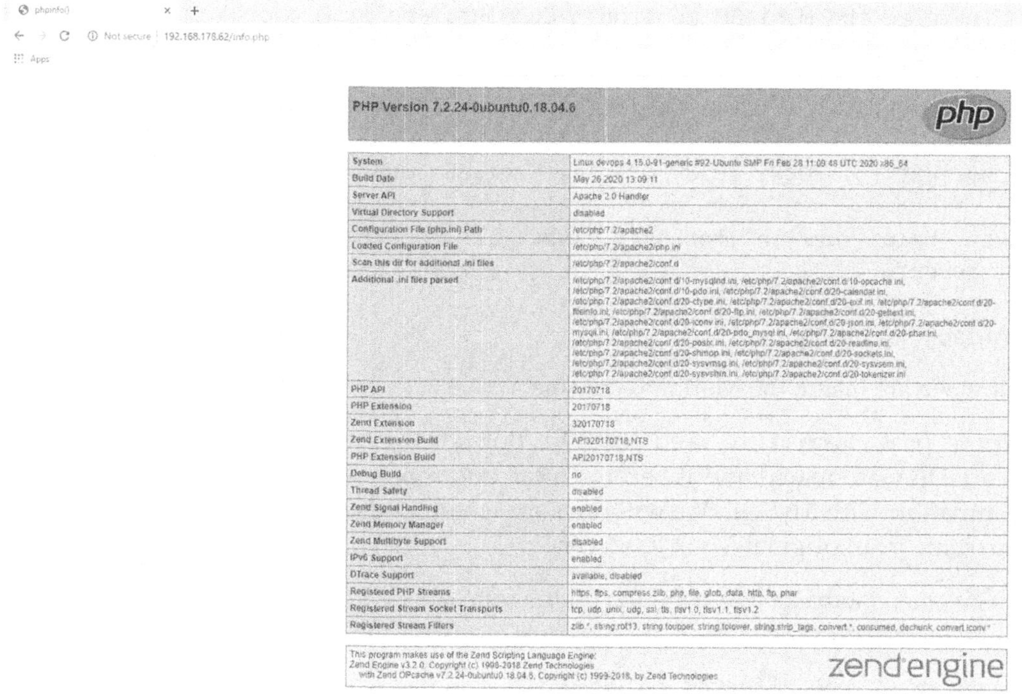

Figure 3.2

Now, you can see via browser, everything which is installed with your PHP installation, and make sure that PHP is running. When we are running a complete application within a web server, PHP and Apache are enough to publish the information and make it available for access everywhere.

However, full systems store and manage data, and in order to do it, we need a **Database Management System**, which can be many. We have as much database systems as we have programming languages, and in different categories, SQL, NoSQL, Key Values, etc.

The most popular DBMS running on web servers is MySQL/MariaDB. So, let's install it and test.

Installing MariaDB

The most popular DBMS running on web servers is the MySQL, then let's install it and make a test:

```
root@devops:~# apt install mariadb-server mariadb-client -y
```

After the installation completes, run the following command:

```
root@devops:~# mysql
Welcome to the MariaDB monitor.  Commands end with ; or \g.
Your MariaDB connection id is 30
Server version: 10.1.44-MariaDB-0ubuntu0.18.04.1 Ubuntu 18.04

Copyright (c) 2000, 2018, Oracle, MariaDB Corporation Ab and others.

Type 'help;' or '\h' for help. Type '\c' to clear the current input
statement.

MariaDB [(none)]>
```

Now we are inside the MariaDB console.

In the past, we usually used MySQL. But, after Oracle bought it, a fork called MariaDB was created and it became more and more popular. Its API is completely compatible with MySQL. We will run some commands here and you can use exactly the same in an original MySQL server.

To create a database, you need to run the following command:

```
MariaDB [(none)]> create database chapter03;
Query OK, 1 row affected (0.00 sec)

MariaDB [(none)]> use chapter03;
Database changed
MariaDB [chapter03]>
```

You can see that we created a database, called `chapter03`, with no tables:

```
MariaDB [chapter03]> show tables;
Empty set (0.00 sec)
```

We can create one by running the following command:

```
MariaDB [chapter03]> create table users( id integer primary key auto_
increment, name varchar(50));
Query OK, 0 rows affected (1.77 sec)
```

We just created a table with 2 columns, one called ID, which will store numbers, and the other called name, which will receive strings. To check the table structure, use the following command:

```
MariaDB [chapter03]>desc users;
```

```
+-------+-------------+------+-----+---------+----------------+
| Field | Type        | Null | Key | Default | Extra          |
+-------+-------------+------+-----+---------+----------------+
| id    | int(11)     | NO   | PRI | NULL    | auto_increment |
| name  | varchar(50) | YES  |     | NULL    |                |
+-------+-------------+------+-----+---------+----------------+
2 rows in set (0.00 sec)
```

Now, we enter some data:

```
MariaDB [chapter03]> insert into users(name) values('alisson');
Query OK, 1 row affected (2.24 sec)


MariaDB [chapter03]> insert into users(name) values('gabriela');
Query OK, 1 row affected (0.11 sec)


MariaDB [chapter03]> insert into users(name) values('juergen');
Query OK, 1 row affected (0.06 sec)


MariaDB [chapter03]> insert into users(name) values('leonardo');
Query OK, 1 row affected (0.06 sec)
```

I just entered 4 different users, alisson, gabriela, juergen, and leonardo to demonstrate how we can see the data stored in a table:

```
MariaDB [chapter03]>select * from users;
```

```
+----+----------+
| id | name     |
+----+----------+
|  1 | alisson  |
```

```
|  2 | gabriela |
|  3 | juergen  |
|  4 | leonardo |
+----+----------+
4 rows in set (0.00 sec)
```

Notice that I just entered the names and the numbers were automatically increased by the database. This is normal when we have an auto-increment column. We did that just to make sure the database server is running. Now, we have a full setup which we call **LAMP (Linux Apache MariaDB PHP)** and we are ready to deploy a real application.

For that, we will use WordPress and see how it works. Leave the MariaDB console by pressing *Ctrl + D*.

Installing WordPress

The first task is to download WordPress from the official website:

```
root@devops:~# wget https://wordpress.org/latest.tar.gz
--2020-07-06 13:51:03--  https://wordpress.org/latest.tar.gz
Resolving wordpress.org (wordpress.org)... 198.143.164.252
Connecting to wordpress.org (wordpress.org)|198.143.164.252|:443...
connected.
HTTP request sent, awaiting response... 200 OK
Length: 12238031 (12M) [application/octet-stream]
Saving to: 'latest.tar.gz'

latest.tar.gz                  100%[=====================
================================================================>]
11.67M   359KB/s    in 31s

2020-07-06 13:51:35 (380 KB/s) - 'latest.tar.gz' saved
[12238031/12238031]
```

Now, you need to decompress the file inside the Apache folder:

```
root@devops:~# tar -xf latest.tar.gz -C /var/www/html/
root@devops:~# ls /var/www/html/
index.html  index.nginx-debian.html  info.php  wordpress
```

See that now we have a WordPress folder within /var/www/html with the following files:

```
root@devops:~# cd /var/www/html/wordpress/
```

```
root@devops:/var/www/html/wordpress# ls
```

index.php   readme.html   wp-admin   wp-comments-post.
php wp-content   wp-includes   wp-load.php   wp-mail.php   wp-
signup.php   xmlrpc.php

license.txt wp-activate.php wp-blog-header.php wp-config-sample.
php wp-cron.php wp-links-opml.php wp-login.php wp-settings.php wp-
trackback.php

The important file is the `wp-config-sample.php`. We will rename it to `wp-config.php` and edit setting the database information for our website. Now, let's do it:

```
root@devops:/var/www/html/wordpress# mv wp-config-sample.php wp-config.php
root@devops:/var/www/html/wordpress# vim wp-config.php
/** The name of the database for WordPress */
define( 'DB_NAME', 'database_name_here' );

/** MySQL database username */
define( 'DB_USER', 'username_here' );

/** MySQL database password */
define( 'DB_PASSWORD', 'password_here' );

/** MySQL hostname */
define( 'DB_HOST', 'localhost' );

/** Database Charset to use in creating database tables. */
define( 'DB_CHARSET', 'utf8' );

/** The Database Collate type. Don't change this if in doubt. */
define( 'DB_COLLATE', '' );
```

Previously, you can see that WordPress is already telling you where you have to replace the values, and then you can edit the file to the following:

```
/** The name of the database for WordPress */
define( 'DB_NAME', 'chapter03' );

/** MySQL database username */
define( 'DB_USER', 'devops' );

/** MySQL database password */
define( 'DB_PASSWORD', 'devops' );

/** MySQL hostname */
define( 'DB_HOST', 'localhost' );
```

With all the credentials and configuration set, we have to create the same on MariaDB:

root@devops:**/var/www/html/wordpress# mariadb**

Welcome to the MariaDB monitor. Commands end with ; or \g.

Your MariaDB connection id is 31

Server version: 10.1.44-MariaDB-0ubuntu0.18.04.1 Ubuntu 18.04

Copyright (c) 2000, 2018, Oracle, MariaDB Corporation Ab and others.

Type 'help;' or '\h' for help. Type '\c' to clear the current input statement.

MariaDB [(none)]> use chapter03

Reading table information for completion of table and column names

You can turn off this feature to get a quicker startup with -A

Database changed

MariaDB [chapter03]> grant all privileges on chapter03.* to devops@'%' identified by 'devops';

Query OK, 0 rows affected (0.00 sec)

We just created a user, called devops and granted all the privileges to all the tables in the chapter03 database. Now, you can access it via browser:

http://192.168.178.62/wordpress

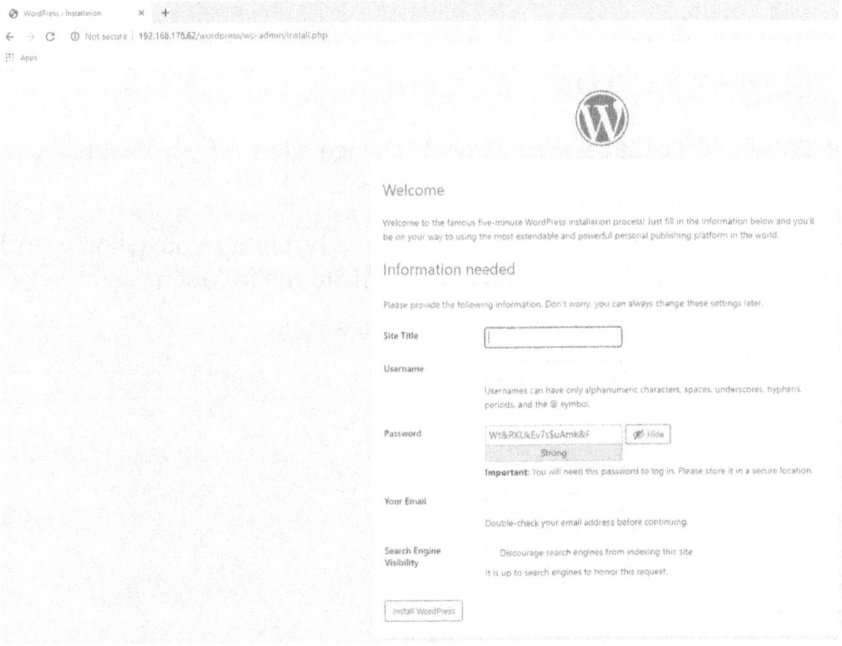

Figure 3.3

You can fill the fields with the following parameters:

Site Title: Chapter03

Username: devops

Password: devops

Click on **Install and finish**, and after that, you need to click on **Login**:

Figure 3.4

Use the same credentials you set earlier, and you will see the WordPress administration:

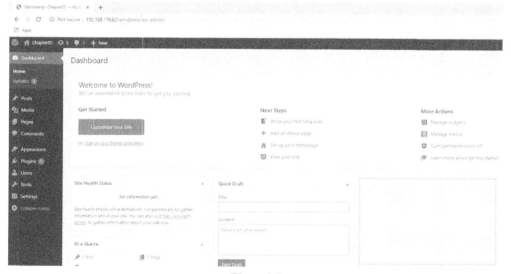

Figure 3.5

Conclusion

We just set up the most popular stack on Linux using PHP, Apache, and MariaDB. If you are working with webhosting or as a freelance web developer, it can be very useful for you, because you can create the websites using WordPress and now you know how to set up and manage your server. It was just a prerequisite for the next chapters where we will automate everything.

CHAPTER 4
Configuring a Reverse Proxy with Nginx

This chapter aims to explain how a reverse proxy is used and what it does. You will also learn how to create a simple page in Python using the framework Flask and make it available using the web server Gunicorn.

Structure

In this chapter, we will discuss the following topics:

- Installing Nginx
- Installing Python
  - Creating a simple page using Flask
- Configuring reverse proxy

Objectives

After studying this unit, you should be able to answer:

- What is Nginx and how it works
- What is a reverse proxy
- The basics of a web page in Python
- How to deploy an application using Gunicorn

Installing the Nginx

Nginx, the name is made up by the sound when you pronounce Engine X. It is also one of the most famous web servers, more frequently used as a load balancer or as a proxy pass. One of its own best capabilities is working with threads to respond a lot of requisitions in parallel. It is frequently used with Python applications. It receives the requisitions and passes to another Python server like Gunicorn, as we will see in the following pages.

To begin with, let's install Nginx by running the following command:

```
root@devops:~# apt install nginx -y
Reading package lists... Done
Building dependency tree
Reading state information... Done
```

The following additional packages will be installed:

```
fontconfig-config fonts-dejavu-core libfontconfig1 libgd3 libjbig0 libjpeg-
turbo8 libjpeg8 libnginx-mod-http-geoip libnginx-mod-http-image-filter

libnginx-mod-http-xslt-filter libnginx-mod-mail libnginx-mod-stream
libtiff5 libwebp6 libxpm4 nginx-common nginx-core
```

Suggested packages:

```
libgd-tools fcgiwrap nginx-doc
```

The following NEW packages will be installed:

```
fontconfig-config fonts-dejavu-core libfontconfig1 libgd3 libjbig0 libjpeg-
turbo8 libjpeg8 libnginx-mod-http-geoip libnginx-mod-http-image-filter

libnginx-mod-http-xslt-filter libnginx-mod-mail libnginx-mod-stream
libtiff5 libwebp6 libxpm4 nginx nginx-common nginx-core

0 upgraded, 18 newly installed, 0 to remove and 72 not upgraded.

Need to get 2,461 kB of archives.
```

After the installation finishes, you can check all the configuration files in this folder by the following command:

```
root@devops:~# ls /etc/nginx/
conf.d           fastcgi_params koi-win     modules-available nginx.conf
scgi_params         sites-enabled  uwsgi_params

fastcgi.conf koi-utf          mime.types modules-enabled      proxy_
params sites-available snippets        win-utf
```

Probably, you saw some similarities with Apache. For example, here also, we have the folder `sites-enable` and `sites-disable`. So, you already know what these directories do. However, the most important is the `nginx.conf.` that stores the main configuration of the web server. We can use the command `grep` to check the enabled lines, in other words, the lines which are not commentaries:

```
root@devops:~# grep -v "#" /etc/nginx/nginx.conf
user www-data;
worker_processes auto;
pid /run/nginx.pid;
include /etc/nginx/modules-enabled/*.conf;

events {
        worker_connections 768;
}

http {

        sendfile on;
        tcp_nopush on;
        tcp_nodelay on;
        keepalive_timeout 65;
        types_hash_max_size 2048;

        include /etc/nginx/mime.types;
        default_type application/octet-stream;

        ssl_prefer_server_ciphers on;

        access_log /var/log/nginx/access.log;
        error_log /var/log/nginx/error.log;

        gzip on;



        include /etc/nginx/conf.d/*.conf;
        include /etc/nginx/sites-enabled/*;

}
```

Therefore, this file can show you the important lines, like the number of connections per worker, so each worker will be in charge to respond **768** connections. By default, the value is 1, but we can have at least one per CPU processor. If you want to check how many processors you have in your CPU, run the following command:

```
root@devops:~# cat /proc/cpuinfo | grep processor
processor       : 0
```

The last command shows you that you have only one processor in your CPU. I ran this command on my VM. Since I have only one processor, if I run in my physical machine, the result is as follows:

```
alisson@avell:~$ cat /proc/cpuinfo  | grep processor
processor       : 0
processor       : 1
processor       : 2
processor       : 3
processor       : 4
processor       : 5
processor       : 6
processor       : 7  show - show package details
```

Therefore, in this case, I can configure my **Nginx** to use 8 workers. If you want to do that, just add the following line below the worker connections:

```
Worker_processes 8;
```

Restart your server and the configuration is enabled.

We just saw some important files. Now is the time to test our web server. In the last chapter, we installed Apache web server in the virtual machine. So, probably it is still running. Let's check if there is any process running on port **80**:

```
root@devops:~# ss -ntpl
State                    Recv-Q              Send-Q
Local Address:Port                           Peer Address:Port

LISTEN                   0                   80
127.0.0.1:3306                               0.0.0.0:*
users:(("mysqld",pid=1100,fd=21))

LISTEN                   0                   128127.0.0.53%lo:53
0.0.0.0:*                       users:(("systemd-resolve",pid=705,fd=13))

LISTEN                   0                   128
0.0.0.0:22                                   0.0.0.0:*
users:(("sshd",pid=942,fd=3))
```

```
LISTEN                  0                           128
*:80                                                *:*
users:(("apache2",pid=3107,fd=4),("apache2",pid=3106,fd=4),("apache2"
,pid=3105,fd=4),("apache2",pid=3104,fd=4),("apache2",pid= 3103,fd=4),("a
pache2",pid=3098,fd=4))
LISTEN                  0                           128
[::]:22                                             [::]:*
users:(("sshd",pid=942,fd=4))
```

The last command is printed on the screen. Of all the services that are currently listening in my VM, if Apache is one of them, let's stop it, disable the server, and start Nginx:

root@devops:~# **systemctl stop apache2**

root@devops:~# **systemctl disable apache2**

```
Synchronizing state of apache2.service with SysV service script with /
lib/systemd/systemd-sysv-install.
```

```
Executing: /lib/systemd/systemd-sysv-install disable apache2
```

Now, even if you restart your VM, Apache will be still stopped. To start and enable Nginx, run the following commands:

root@devops:~# **systemctl start nginx**

root@devops:~# **systemctl enable nginx**

```
Synchronizing state of nginx.service with SysV service script with /lib/
systemd/systemd-sysv-install.
```

```
Executing: /lib/systemd/systemd-sysv-install enable nginx
```

Open the IP address in the browser to check the index page: http://192.168.178.62/:

Figure 4.1

It is interesting that it is displaying the Apache example page. This happens because Nginx is using the same folder as Apache for the document root. You can check that using the following command:

root@devops:~# **grep -v "#" /etc/nginx/sites-enabled/default**

```
server {
    listen 80 default_server;
    listen [::]:80 default_server;

    root /var/www/html;

    index index.html index.htm index.nginx-debian.html;

    server_name _;

    location / {
        try_files $uri $uri/ =404;
    }

}
```

The grep command showed you that the document root is defined as /var/www/ html, which is the same as Apache. If you want to see the default index page of Nginx, run the following command:

root@devops:~# **cp -v /usr/share/nginx/html/index.html /var/www/html/**

'/usr/share/nginx/html/index.html' -> '/var/www/html/index.html'

The grep command showed you that the document root is defined as /var/www/ html, which is the same as Apache. If you want to see the default index page of the Nginx, run the following command:

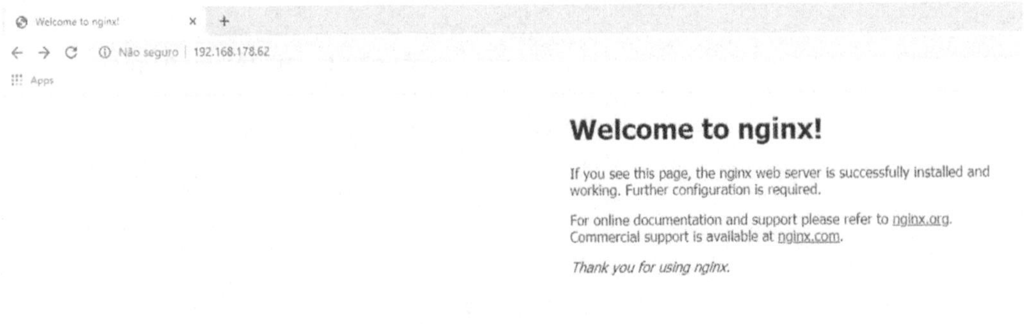

Figure 4.2

Now, you can see the Nginx default page.

Installing Python

Python, nowadays, is one of the most famous programming languages, mainly in the areas, like Data Science and DevOps. It is frequently used to automate Linux tasks and integrate systems using REST APIs. Some years ago, I worked in a system called BeavOps. I was responsible to make the enrollment of the students for the consulting company I used to work for.

That system was receiving a JSON file from the CRM with the student data, the respective course, and the starting and ending date. The mission was to create some routines with this data which will integrate many different tools, like Gitlab, Jenkins, Apache, MongoDB, etc, aiming to create a development environment for the students and with a CI/CD pipeline. That system was completely made up using Python, Flask, and MongoDB to store the data.

To install Python, we basically need two packages:

```
root@devops:~# apt install python3 python3-pip -y
Reading package lists... Done
Building dependency tree
Reading state information... Done
python3 is already the newest version (3.6.7-1~18.04).
python3 set to manually installed.
```

So, the options are self-explained. Therefore, let's use them in practice. After the installation finishes, install the Flask framework using `pip`:

```
root@devops:~# python3 -m pip install flask
Collecting flask
  Downloading https://files.pythonhosted.org/
packages/9b/93/628509b8d5dc749656a9641f4caf13540e2cdec85276964ff8f43bbb
1d3b/Flask-1.1.1-py2.py3-none-any.whl (94kB)
     100% |████████████████████████████████| 102kB 1.4MB/s
```

Now, your environment is ready to run a Python application.

Creating a simple page using Flask

Flask is a micro-framework for Python, which is perfect for you to create your APIs. Now, you will learn how to create a simple `Hello World` using this micro-framework and Python. You will also learn all the steps to deploy your application using Nginx and Gunicorn.

Let's create a file, called app.py with the following content:

```
from flask import Flask

app = Flask(__name__)

@app.route("/")
def index():
    return "DevOps with Linux"

if __name__ == "__main__":
    app.run(debug=True,host="0.0.0.0")
```

Now, run the following command:

```
root@devops:~# python3 app.py
 * Serving Flask app "app" (lazy loading)
 * Environment: production
   WARNING: This is a development server. Do not use it in a production
deployment.
   Use a production WSGI server instead.
 * Debug mode: on
 * Running on http://0.0.0.0:5000/ (Press CTRL+C to quit)
 * Restarting with stat
 * Debugger is active!
 * Debugger PIN: 179-281-442
```

Now, you can see the internal server running. Like we used PHP, the same is applied to Python, and then you can get your IP address. Access from your web browser and you must see a page like that the one following:

Figure 4.3

As the log from the Flask says by itself, this server is just for the development purposes. We must use a **WSGI (Web Server Gateway Interface)**. If you want to learn more about that, you can access the PEP 333 page: **https://www.python.org/dev/peps/pep-0333/**. It explains more details about that topic, but for now, our focus is to deploy the application.

The WSGI server that we will use will be Gunicorn. It is just one of the many options that are available. To install it, run the following command:

```
root@devops:~# python3 -m pip install gunicorn
Collecting gunicorn
  Downloading https://files.pythonhosted.org/packages/69/
ca/926f7cd3a2014b16870086b2d0fdc84a9e49473c68a8dff8b57f7c156f43/
gunicorn-20.0.4-py2.py3-none-any.whl (77kB)
     100% |████████████████████████████████| 81kB 1.3MB/s
Requirement already satisfied: setuptools>=3.0 in /usr/lib/python3/dist-
packages (from gunicorn)
Installing collected packages: gunicorn
Successfully installed gunicorn-20.0.4
```

Now, we can deploy the application again, but using the WSGI server. To do this, run the following command:

```
root@devops:~# gunicorn --chdir /root/ app:app -b "0.0.0.0"
[2020-03-23 18:34:13 +0000] [23783] [INFO] Starting gunicorn 20.0.4
[2020-03-23 18:34:13 +0000] [23783] [INFO] Listening at:
http://0.0.0.0:8000 (23783)
[2020-03-23 18:34:13 +0000] [23783] [INFO] Using worker: sync
[2020-03-23 18:34:13 +0000] [23786] [INFO] Booting worker with pid:
23786
```

Notice that the port has changed. Now, you must use the port **8000**:

Figure 4.4

It's so simple like that. However, we also want to run this application behind a reverse proxy. So, let's see how we are going to configure that.

Configuring the Reverse Proxy

We have already installed Nginx in our VM and we also know the configuration files. Knowing that, the configuration for the pages can be found in the virtual hosts which are found in the directory:

```
root@devops:~# ls /etc/nginx/sites-available/default
```

```
/etc/nginx/sites-available/default
```

Then, we can open the file and your file should have the content as follows:

```
server {
    listen 80 default_server;
    listen [::]:80 default_server;

    server_name _;

    location / {
        proxy_pass http://localhost:8000/ ;
    }

}
```

Restart the server to enable the configuration:

```
root@devops:~# systemctl restart nginx
root@devops:~#
```

If you try to access the server using the default port 80, you will see the following message:

Figure 4.5

It happens because the server behind our proxy is not running yet. So, let's run it and check the changes:

```
root@devops:~# gunicorn --chdir /root/ app:app
[2020-03-23 18:52:26 +0000] [24025] [INFO] Starting gunicorn 20.0.4
[2020-03-23 18:52:26 +0000] [24025] [INFO] Listening at:
http://127.0.0.1:8000 (24025)
[2020-03-23 18:52:26 +0000] [24025] [INFO] Using worker: sync
[2020-03-23 18:52:26 +0000] [24028] [INFO] Booting worker with pid:
24028
```

This time we do not need to pass the bind option, -b to make the server available to all the IP address. In the current case, the server is just listening to the localhost. Therefore, Nginx is open to the world receiving the connections and forwarding it to Gunicorn.

If you try to access again using the default port, you will see that now we are able to see the service run:

Figure 4.6

The environment is ready. Reverse proxies are used for many strategies. One of the most common is caching the static files, like JavaScript, CSS, and HTML. Therefore, all the incoming connections are responded by Nginx and only the dynamic content is forwarded to Gunicorn. This way is less costly for the CPU to process everything. In the future chapters, we will see how to apply the same logic, but using the Cloud services, which are the most common today. But, if you are using on-premises infrastructure, this can be a good strategy to increase the performance.

CHAPTER 5
Deploying Your Application Using Docker

This chapter aims to explain how to install Docker, how to work using it, create new containers, images, networks, and deploy the image inside a server.

Structure

In this chapter, we will discuss the following topics:

- Introduction to Docker
- Installing Docker and creating containers
- Creating images using Dockerfile
- Publishing images and deploying it

Objectives

After studying this unit, you should be able to:

- Understand what is Docker and how it works
- Setup a Docker environment
- Create containers and images
- Version images and deploying

Introduction to Docker

Docker is a tool set to create containers and version it. For those who have more experience with Linux, they probably already know what a container is by using the command `chroot` on Linux. In simple words, a container is a directory in your file system that allows you to install another Linux operating system in it. As the command says `chroot` (change `root`), so the new root directory /, will be the new one that you set. However, an entire operating system needs so much more than just the files. Then, for the networking part, the Docker uses iptables under the hood. To manage some redirects via NAT rules, I will show you the amount of stuff that Docker manages for you by running some simple commands in the following paragraphs.

Installation

Firstly, we need to install Docker in our environment. In the official documentation, you will find all the steps and the detailed instructions. Here, we have a summary of everything:

```
apt clean
```

```
apt-get update
```

```
apt-get remove docker docker-engine docker.io containerd runc -y
```

The preceding commands will remove any previous installation of Docker, if you had one in your machine:

```
apt-get install apt-transport-https ca-certificates curl gnupg-agent
software-properties-common -y
```

Now, we are just installing some dependencies that are required for your Docker installation, like the `apt-transport-https`, which is a requirement to download packages from the `https` repositories:

```
curl -fsSL https://download.docker.com/linux/ubuntu/gpg | apt-key add -
```

The following command will add **GNU Privacy Guard** key to ensure the authenticity of the Docker repository:

```
add-apt-repository "deb [arch=amd64] https://download.docker.com/linux/
ubuntu $(lsb_release -cs) stable"
```

We are using Ubuntu. So, the preceding command is specifically for Ubuntu environments:

```
apt-get update -y
```

```
apt-get install docker-ce docker-ce-cli containerd.io -y
```

To conclude, the previous command were to update your local repositories list and install the Docker Community Edition.

Creating Containers

The environment is ready. To ensure that your Docker is running fine, run the following command:

```
root@devops:~# systemctl status docker

    docker.service - Docker Application Container Engine

    Loaded: loaded (/lib/systemd/system/docker.service; enabled; vendor
    preset: enabled)

    Active: active (running) since Thu 2020-04-02 10:28:47 UTC; 1min 7s
    ago

    Docs: https://docs.docker.com
Main PID: 6464 (dockerd)

    Tasks: 9

CGroup: /system.slice/docker.service

    └─6464 /usr/bin/dockerd -H fd:// --containerd=/run/containerd/
containerd.sock
```

Now, your Docker installation is active and running. To create one container, you can just type the following command:

```
root@devops:~# docker run -ti centos /bin/bash

Unable to find image 'centos:latest' locally

latest: Pulling from library/centos

8a29a15cefae: Downloading [=============================================
====> ]  72.58MB/73.23MB
```

The previous command means that we need to run a new container with a TTY (terminal), which is represented by the parameter -t, and an interactive, represented by the parameter -i. Thus, we can run the commands in the container terminal and see their outputs.

When your container is created, you can see the following output:

```
root@devops:~# docker run -ti centos /bin/bash

Unable to find image 'centos:latest' locally

latest: Pulling from library/centos

8a29a15cefae: Pull complete
        Digest:
```

```
sha256:fe8d824220415eed5477b63addf40fb06c3b049404242b31982106ac204f6700
Status: Downloaded newer image for centos:latest
[root@595b42fceebc /]#
```

The last line is the important one:

```
[root@595b42fceebc /]#
```

If you compare with our terminal in before running the command:

root@devops:~# docker run -ti centos /bin/bash

You can clearly see that the hostname is changed, which means now we are within the container and all the commands we will run, starting from now, will be running inside the container, and nothing will be installed in the VM environment. The hostname name given to the container 595b42fceebc is the container ID, which is used to manage your container. To exit from your container, type: exit or *Ctrl + D*:

```
[root@595b42fceebc /]#
exit
root@devops:~#
```

To see your current running containers, type the following command:

root@devops:~# **docker container ls**

CONTAINER ID	IMAGE	COMMAND	CREATED
STATUS	PORTS	NAMES	

We can see zero containers running. It happens because once you type exit or *Ctrl + D* from your container terminal, the container stops. To see that, type the following command:

root@devops:~# **docker container ls -a**

CONTAINER ID	IMAGE		COMMAND		CREATED
STATUS		PORTS		NAMES	
595b42fceebc	centos		"/bin/bash"		9 minutes
ago	Exited (0) 2 minutes ago				hardcore_
neumann					

Now, you can see your container created. If you give a look, you can see that the value in the column CONTAINER ID is exactly the same as the container hostname when we created it.

However, why does the Docker has this behavior? Why is it that when we exit from a container, the container stops? This happens because in the containers concept, one container is created for one specific purpose, different from the virtual machines. So, we do not need to concern about uptime or maintaining a container. You can just delete it and create a new one. If you want to make changes into a container, you must modify the image, save it, delete the current container, and start a new one with the new version of the image.

In my case, I created a container based on a CentOS image, and I just ran the command `/bin/bash`, which was keeping my container alive. Once that command stops running, the container becomes dead. It also applies for the container configurations. If you want to change a redirect or any other parameters, you must create a new container with those new parameters, save it, and run a new container.

Now, we will create a new container based in the CentOS image, and within this container, we will put a Python application that we learned in the last chapter:

```
root@devops:~# docker run -ti --name python_app -p 5000:5000 centos /
bin/bash
[root@ce7f74b0304a /]#
```

The creation now was clearly faster than the first one. This happens because the CentOS image is already in our local repository. Therefore, the Docker does not need to download it again.

Install the dependencies in the container with the following command:

```
[root@ce7f74b0304a /]# yum clean all && yum install python3 python3-pip
-y
Failed to set locale, defaulting to C.UTF-8
0 files removed
Failed to set locale, defaulting to C.UTF-8
CentOS-8 - AppStream                                             11%
[=======                                                    ] 122
kB/s | 767 kB      00:49 ETA
```

While the download is running, we have a new command now, the `yum`. This command is respective to APT on Ubuntu, and you can use it to install the packages from remote repositories.

After the download finishes, install the Python modules for the application:

```
[root@ce7f74b0304a /]# python3 -m pip install flask
Successfully installed Jinja2-2.11.1 MarkupSafe-1.1.1 Werkzeug-1.0.1
click-7.1.1 flask-1.1.1 itsdangerous-1.1.0
```

Copy the source code used in the previous chapter to the container:

```
[root@ce7f74b0304a /]# cat <<EOF > /srv/app.py
> from flask import Flask
>
```

```
> app = Flask(__name__)
>
> @app.route("/")
> def index():
>       return "DevOps with Linux"
>
>
> if __name__ == "__main__":
>       app.run(debug=True,host="0.0.0.0")
> EOF
```

Run the application to see if it is working:

```
[root@ce7f74b0304a /]# python3 /srv/app.py
* Serving Flask app "app" (lazy loading)
* Environment: production
WARNING: This is a development server. Do not use it in a production
deployment.
Use a production WSGI server instead.
* Debug mode: on
* Running on http://0.0.0.0:5000/ (Press CTRL+C to quit)
* Restarting with stat
* Debugger is active!
* Debugger PIN: 123-083-749
```

Perfect! Now, you can test if from the web browser:

DevOps with Linux

Figure 5.1

Everything is running fine. Now, we have a container running, with an application inside it. The dependencies were installed and we already know the command to run the application. Now, we need to create a new image based on this one. To create the image, we need to exit the container. So, let's do it:

[root@ce7f74b0304a /]# python3 /srv/app.py

* Serving Flask app "app" (lazy loading)

* Environment: production

WARNING: This is a development server. Do not use it in a production deployment.

Use a production WSGI server instead.

* Debug mode: on

* Running on http://0.0.0.0:5000/ (Press CTRL+C to quit)

* Restarting with stat

* Debugger is active!

* Debugger PIN: 123-083-749

192.168.178.60 - - [02/Apr/2020 11:08:54] "GET / HTTP/1.1" 200 -

192.168.178.60 - - [02/Apr/2020 11:08:54] "GET /favicon.ico HTTP/1.1" 404 -

[root@ce7f74b0304a /]# exit

root@devops:~#

The important lines are the last ones, where I type *Ctrl + C* to stop the application, and *Ctrl + D* to exit the container:

```
root@devops:~# docker container ls -a
CONTAINER ID        IMAGE           COMMAND          CREATED
STATUS                      PORTS               NAMES
ce7f74b0304a        centos          "/bin/bash"         18 minutes
ago       Exited (0) 57 seconds ago                python_app
595b42fceebc        centos          "/bin/bash"         38 minutes
ago       Exited (0) 30 minutes ago                hardcore_
neumann
```

We now have one container, called python_app. If you check the last column, this is the one we wanted to create an image:

root@devops:~# **docker commit python_app my_first_image**

```
sha256:866e933c059b90a098cad06a1989d24bf16870caea1d691e2c0d3f4599f1608c
```

The parameter commit receives the first parameter as one container; it can be a running container or a stopped container, it does not matter; and the second parameter is the image name. Therefore, we are creating a new image called my_first_image.

You can check the images that you have running by the following command:

```
root@devops:~# docker image ls
```

REPOSITORY SIZE	TAG	IMAGE ID	CREATED
my_first_image ago279MB	latest	866e933c059b	2 minutes
centos 237MB	latest	470671670cac	2 months ago

We can see two images; one is the CentOS image that we downloaded from the Docker Hub, which is the official repository. The other one is my_first_image that we created just now. You can create many instances of your application that you want just by running the following command:

```
root@devops:~# docker run -ti -p 5000:5000 my_first_image python3 /srv/
app.py
* Serving Flask app "app" (lazy loading)
* Environment: production
WARNING: This is a development server. Do not use it in a production
deployment.
Use a production WSGI server instead.
* Debug mode: on
* Running on http://0.0.0.0:5000/ (Press CTRL+C to quit)
* Restarting with stat
```

The parameter -p 5000:5000, is mapping the port 5000 from our local machine to the port 5000 of our container.

If you want to publish your image to download into any other server, you can create an account in the Docker Hub **https://hub.docker.com/**, and send your image there. In my case, I already have an account, so I will teach you how to send your own image to the hub:

```
root@devops:~# docker login
Login with your Docker ID to push and pull images from Docker Hub. If
you don't have a Docker ID, head over to https://hub.docker.com to
create one.
```

```
Username: alissonmenezes

Password:

WARNING! Your password will be stored unencrypted in /root/.docker/
config.json.

Configure a credential helper to remove this warning. See

https://docs.docker.com/engine/reference/commandline/login/#credentials-
store


Login Succeeded
```

The username is what you defined while creating the account. You must use the Docker login, to authenticate into your repository. The username is also used to specify where you will store that image, for example:

```
root@devops:~# docker tag my_first_image alissonmenezes/my_first_image
root@devops:~# docker push alissonmenezes/my_first_image
The push refers to repository [docker.io/alissonmenezes/my_first_image]
ef02c4bc0109: Pushing [=======================
====>                   ]  22.67MB/41.69MB
ef02c4bc0109: Pushed
```

Now, my image is published for the whole world. If I check my own profile on Docker Hub, I can see the following:

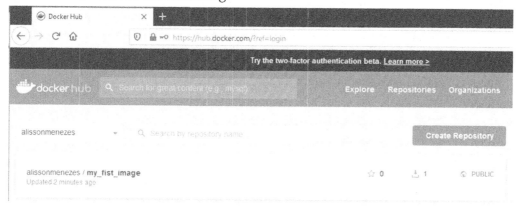

Figure 5.2

My image is saved and is prepared to run on any Docker installed around the world. So now, I will clean my environment, all the images and containers, and create a new container based on that image downloaded directly from the hub:

```
root@devops:~# docker system prune
WARNING! This will remove:
```

- all stopped containers

- all networks not used by at least one container

- all dangling images

- all dangling build cache

Are you sure you want to continue? [y/N] y

Deleted Containers:

06035663ec0423a479cddb0c287637626641c79c93896c6566efb802dc3ea35f

4bbab42a400fc72a339977886cde2e061c9c1dce78305d5cb56336e6f36d5965

adc48c7c0be4d422891b9e44146018c175120aab202a338f88f4a1847b50ba67

ce7f74b0304a9bc08bf0ccdd2832d6907408c0f6a9c80c56a75d3bdbf6738b62

595b42fceebc9e4f9c6e2d23d54a8ecd7eaead266ef114c953b1715d0f58a7ee

Total reclaimed space: 41.69MB

The command, docker system prune is used to clean your environment, deleting all the stopped containers. I will run that and let's validate if the environment is cleaned:

root@devops:~# **docker container ls -a**

CONTAINER ID	IMAGE	COMMAND	CREATED
STATUS	PORTS	NAMES	

No containers running. Now, let's delete all the images:

root@devops:~# **docker image rm $(docker image ls)**

Untagged: alissonmenezes/my_fist_image:latest

Untagged: alissonmenezes/my_fist_image@
sha256:3c729fd3e1a595ff2bcf0937611732550ebde0c0d1945a87c01f979ca620b9fa

Untagged: my_first_image:latest

Deleted:
sha256:866e933c059b90a098cad06a1989d24bf16870caea1d691e2c0d3f4599f1608c

Deleted:
sha256:fbf13ca6b28b7113d750e70b57c59e2cfc90ae6b3c7436166161c92eef1dc219

Untagged: centos:latest

Checking if we still have images:

root@devops:~# **docker image ls -a**

REPOSITORY	TAG	IMAGE ID	CREATED
SIZE			

No images. Let's create a container based on the image that we pushed to the hub:

```
root@devops:~# docker run -ti -p 5000:5000 alissonmenezes/my_fist_
image:latest python3 /srv/app.py
Unable to find image 'alissonmenezes/my_fist_image:latest' locally
latest: Pulling from alissonmenezes/my_fist_image
8a29a15cefae: Pull complete
        f21402989f68: Pull complete
        Digest:
sha256:3c729fd3e1a595ff2bcf0937611732550ebde0c0d1945a87c01f979ca620b9fa
Status: Downloaded newer image for alissonmenezes/my_fist_image:latest
* Serving Flask app "app" (lazy loading)
* Environment: production
WARNING: This is a development server. Do not use it in a production
deployment.
Use a production WSGI server instead.
* Debug mode: on
* Running on http://0.0.0.0:5000/ (Press CTRL+C to quit)
* Restarting with stat
* Debugger is active!
* Debugger PIN: 249-372-527
```

You can now see that the main objective of Docker is to create images for application purposes using an entire environment. We just created a version of CentOS with Python3 installed, and an application inside it. If you want to create a new version of your application, or update the CentoOS version, or even change the underlying OS, like migrating from CentOS to Alpine, you can do that. Do all the tests, create a new version of the image with the same name, send it to the hub, and download it in to your production/quality/development environment.

Creating Images with Dockerfile

Now that you already know all the steps of how to create an image and how to push it into the hub, we can automate these steps using the Dockerfile. This file helps you to track the modifications made into an image. When you just create a container, install everything and create an image. It is a difficult task to track everything that was installed. Therefore, if you want to create a new version for the same application, you have to track all the dependencies and everything, to ensure that all the earlier dependencies are still present in the new image.

Now, create a file, called Dockerfile, and we will include all the steps running in the container within the file:

```
root@devops:~# vim Dockerfile
from centos
maintainer alisson.copyleft@gmail.com

run yum clean all
run yum install python3 python3-pip -y
run python3 -m pip install flask
copy app.py /srv/app.py

expose 5000

cmd ["python3","/srv/app.py"]
```

Earlier, you have the file content, which has exactly all the commands that we ran within the container. The statements are self-explained, thus, you can use:

- from, to specify the base image.
- maintainer, to specify who is maintaining the image.
- run, will execute the commands within the container.
- copy, copy one file from the local machine to the container.
- expose, publishes the container port.
- cmd, the command which will ensure the container running.

To create the image based on Dockerfile, run the following command:

```
root@devops:~# docker build . -t my_new_image
Sending build context to Docker daemon  735.7kB
Step 1/8 : from centos
latest: Pulling from library/centos
8a29a15cefae: Pulling fs layer
```

The Docker build will look for a Dockerfile inside the current directory. The parameter -t means TAG, which will define the image name. So, after the command finishes, you can just create a new container by running the following command:

```
Successfully built b1b23966bb89
Successfully tagged my_new_image:latest
root@devops:~# docker run my_new_image
* Serving Flask app "app" (lazy loading)
* Environment: production
```

```
WARNING: This is a development server. Do not use it in a production
deployment.
```

Use a production WSGI server instead.

* Debug mode: on

* Running on http://0.0.0.0:5000/ (Press CTRL+C to quit)

* Restarting with stat

* Debugger is active!

* Debugger PIN: 130-050-890

It easy to see that now we did not have to pass any additional parameters, because all of them were already passed in the Dockerfile. The Dockerfile basically did the same steps for us before it created a new container. If you check the output, you will see the following:

Successfully built b1b23966bb89

This is the container ID, and in the end the container was tagged with the name specified in the Docker build:

Successfully tagged my_new_image:latest

You can directly put the repository name and push it there. Now, you already know the basics of Docker and it is the minimum requirement for you start to Dockerize your applications.

Conclusion

To conclude, we could see that working with Docker is an easy task. We just have to apply our previous knowledge in a different area of work. Then, you can create a version of your environment, including Infrastructure as Code, ship it to everywhere you want to, but Docker, in itself, is not enough for the large production environments. For that, we have a chapter about Kubernetes and Docker is a requirement for us to work with it.

CHAPTER 6

Automating Your Infrastructure as Code

This chapter aims to explain how the Infrastructure as Code works, install Vagrant, how to work using it, create new virtual machines in an automated way using the Shell Script, and set up all Infrastructure we did before.

Structure

In this chapter, we will discuss the following topics:

- Introduction to Infrastructure as Code
- Installing Vagrant and creating virtual machines
- Setting up a LAMP server
- Setting up a Docker server

Objectives

After studying this unit, you should be able to:

- What is Vagrant and how it works
- Setup a Docker environment using Vagrant automation
- Setting up an Apache server
- Benefits of automation

Introduction to Infrastructure as Code

Infrastructure as Code is a technique used to document, version, and maintain the control of your infrastructure in a very similar way as you do with software development. Then, you can create a file describing the desired state of your infrastructure, deploy it on a test environment, validate your code, deploy on a staging environment, and if everything goes well, you can proceed to the production environment. It is possible using pipelines; therefore, you can use the same code for all the environment and change the server's sizes using the variables defined for each of the environments.

What is Vagrant and How It Works?

In the beginning of this book, you will learn how to setup the VirtualBox, download an ISO, create a VM, attach the ISO, and format and install the operating system. However, it is a recurrent task in the daily life of a DevOps engineer. Can you imagine yourself installing 100 VMs every day and destroying them after the working day to save money? It is insane. But, when we use Infrastructure as Code (IaC), this task becomes very easy to do, because you just need to do some clicks, and run some commands to create and destroy everything.

Vagrant is a tool that can be integrated with the Virtual Box. It is responsible to read your code, convert it into Virtual Box commands, and also run the code within the VM. You need not to execute all those steps learned in the first chapter. HashiCorp created Vagrant and they have an official repository of images that you can use to setup your environment. So, you do not need to go to the official website, download the ISO, and setup the machine.

Vagrant installing

You can download Vagrant from the following link:

https://www.vagrantup.com/downloads.html

I am using Windows, so I will download the MSI version.

Download Vagrant

Below are the available downloads for the latest version of Vagrant (2.2.7). Please download the proper package for your operating system and architecture.

You can find the SHA256 checksums for Vagrant 2.2.7 online and you can verify the checksum's signature file , which has been signed using HashiCorp's GPG key. You can also download older versions of Vagrant from the releases service.

Check out the v2.2.7 CHANGELOG for information on the latest release.

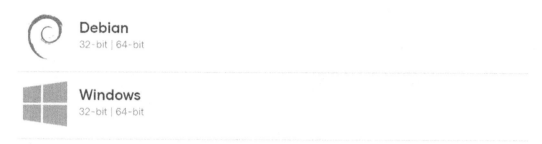

Debian
32-bit | 64-bit

Windows
32-bit | 64-bit

Figure 6.1

The installation process is simple like any other software to be installed on Windows. You just need to open the MSI file and follow the process, **Next**, **Next**:

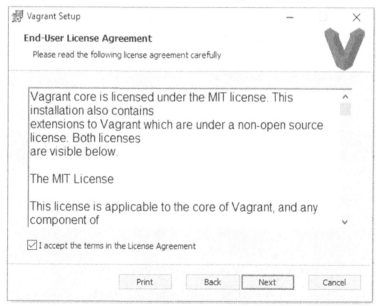

Figure 6.2

And then, click **Finish** with all the default options:

Figure 6.3

Now, since the installation is completed, let us learn the basics.

Usage

Firstly, create a folder to store your vagrant files as I did:

```
PS C:\Users\1511 MXTI>mkdir VagrantChapter


    Directory: C:\Users\1511 MXTI


Mode                 LastWriteTime         Length Name
----                 -------------         ------ ----
d-----        4/13/2020  11:17 AM                VagrantChapter


PS C:\Users\1511 MXTI> cd .\VagrantChapter\
PS C:\Users\1511 MXTI\VagrantChapter>
```

I created a folder, called VagrantChaper and I entered that folder. Right now, it is empty. To create your first code, type the following command:

```
PS C:\Users\1511 MXTI\VagrantChapter> vagrant init
A 'Vagrantfile' has been placed in this directory. You are now
```

ready to 'vagrant up' your first virtual environment! Please read
the comments in the Vagrantfile as well as documentation on
'vagrantup.com' for more information on using Vagrant.
PS C:\Users\1511 MXTI\VagrantChapter>

The command vagrant init, creates a sample file for you with the common
configuration for the most of the cases of VMs. Let's have a look in the file content:

```
PS C:\Users\1511 MXTI\VagrantChapter> cat .\Vagrantfile
# -*- mode: ruby -*-
# vi: set ft=ruby :

# All Vagrant configuration is done below. The "2" in Vagrant.configure
# configures the configuration version (we support older styles for
# backwards compatibility). Please don't change it unless you know what
# you're doing.
Vagrant.configure("2") do |config|
  # The most common configuration options are documented and commented below.
  # For a complete reference, please see the online documentation at
  # https://docs.vagrantup.com.

  # Every Vagrant development environment requires a box. You can search for
  # boxes at https://vagrantcloud.com/search.
  config.vm.box = "base"

  # Disable automatic box update checking. If you disable this, then
  # boxes will only be checked for updates when the user runs
  # 'vagrant box outdated'. This is not recommended.
  # config.vm.box_check_update = false

  # Create a forwarded port mapping which allows access to a specific port
  # within the machine from a port on the host machine. In the example below,
  # accessing "localhost:8080" will access port 80 on the guest machine.
  # NOTE: This will enable public access to the opened port
  # config.vm.network "forwarded_port", guest: 80, host: 8080

  # Create a forwarded port mapping which allows access to a specific port
```

```
# within the machine from a port on the host machine and only allow access
# via 127.0.0.1 to disable public access
# config.vm.network "forwarded_port", guest: 80, host: 8080, host_ip:
"127.0.0.1"

# Create a private network, which allows host-only access to the machine
# using a specific IP.
# config.vm.network "private_network", ip: "192.168.33.10"

# Create a public network, which generally matched to bridged network.
# Bridged networks make the machine appear as another physical device on
# your network.
# config.vm.network "public_network"

# Share an additional folder to the guest VM. The first argument is
# the path on the host to the actual folder. The second argument is
# the path on the guest to mount the folder. And the optional third
# argument is a set of non-required options.
# config.vm.synced_folder "../data", "/vagrant_data"

# Provider-specific configuration so you can fine-tune various
# backing providers for Vagrant. These expose provider-specific options.
# Example for VirtualBox:
#
# config.vm.provider "virtualbox" do |vb|
#   # Display the VirtualBox GUI when booting the machine
#   vb.gui = true
#
#   # Customize the amount of memory on the VM:
#   vb.memory = "1024"
# end
#
# View the documentation for the provider you are using for more
# information on available options.

# Enable provisioning with a shell script. Additional provisioners such as
```

```
  # Ansible, Chef, Docker, Puppet and Salt are also available. Please
see the
  # documentation for more information about their specific syntax and use.
  # config.vm.provision "shell", inline: <<-SHELL
  #    apt-get update
  #    apt-get install -y apache2
  # SHELL
end
```

In the same folder, you run the following command:

```
PS C:\Users\1511 MXTI\VagrantChapter> vagrant status
Current machine states:

default                    not created (virtualbox)
```

It means that we have one VM, called default, and it is not created yet. So, we will create one.

The sample file has some configurations and many comments giving a brief explanation of what the commands do. This file, with the default configuration, allows you to create just one VM. In this chapter, we will create two virtual machines, one with the LAMP server installed, and other with the Docker installed. I will modify that file and explain the differences between the example file and the new one:

```
# -*- mode: ruby -*-
# vi: set ft=ruby :
Vagrant.configure("2") do |config|
  config.vm.box = "ubuntu/focal64"
  config.vm.box_check_update = false
  config.vm.provider "virtualbox" do |vb|
    vb.memory = "1024"
  end

  config.vm.define "lamp" do |lamp|
    lamp.vm.network "private_network", ip: "192.168.33.10"
    lamp.vm.provision "shell", inline: <<-SHELL
      apt-get clean
      apt update -y
    SHELL
```

```
  end

  config.vm.define "docker" do |docker|
    docker.vm.network "private_network", ip: "192.168.33.11"
    docker.vm.provision "shell", inline: <<-SHELL
      apt-get clean
      apt update -y
    SHELL
  end

  config.vm.provision "shell", inline: <<-SHELL
    apt-get clean
    apt update -y
  SHELL

End
```

The preceding file is my new and modified one. It is cleaner than the example one, and does more stuff. Let's run the `vagrant status`, to see if something has changed:

```
PS C:\Users\1511 MXTI\VagrantChapter> vagrant status

Current machine states:

lamp                      not created (virtualbox)
docker                    not created (virtualbox)
```

Interestingly, now we have two virtual machines, one is called a **lamp,** and the other is called Docker. Both are not created yet. In the new file, I used a Vagrant resource called multi-machine. It allows you to create more than one machine per file. So, you can have as many machines as you want in the same file.

Now, let's analyze the file and what will happen before we create the VMs:

```
config.vm.box = "ubuntu/focal64"
  config.vm.box_check_update = false
  config.vm.provider "virtualbox" do |vb|
    vb.memory = "1024"
  end
```

This part with `config.vm` is the common configuration for all the virtual machines declared in the file. So, all the machines will be created with 1024 MB of RAM. The `config.vm.box` is the image which will be used in the machine. In our case, we will use the Ubuntu server, version 20.04:

```
config.vm.define "lamp" do |lamp|
    lamp.vm.network "private_network", ip: "192.168.33.10"
    lamp.vm.provision "shell", inline: <<-SHELL
      apt-get clean
      apt update -y
    SHELL
end
```

In this part, we have a local configuration just for the machine **lamp**. It is specifically for the virtual machine, called lamp. Then, in this called, the VM will have the IP address 192.168.33.10, and the command which will be run in the provision of the VM, as in, inside this part: lamp.vm.provision. It also applies to the Docker VM:

```
config.vm.provision "shell", inline: <<-SHELL
    apt-get clean
    apt update -y
  SHELL
```

In the final part, we have the config.vm.provision. Inside this block, you can define the command which will run in all the VMs, except lamp.vm.provision, which will run only in the lamp VM, and docker.vm.provision, which will run only in the Docker VM. Therefore, we have global configurations that will run in all VMs and local configurations that will run only in the specified VMs.

Up and running

With the file explained and everything configures to create the VMs, type the following command:

```
PS C:\Users\1511 MXTI\VagrantChapter> vagrant up --provider=virtualbox
Bringing machine 'lamp' up with 'virtualbox' provider...
Bringing machine 'docker' up with 'virtualbox' provider...
==> lamp: Box 'ubuntu/focal64' could not be found. Attempting to find and
install...
    lamp: Box Provider: virtualbox
    lamp: Box Version: >= 0
==> lamp: Loading metadata for box 'ubuntu/focal64'
    lamp: URL: https://vagrantcloud.com/ubuntu/focal64
```

It will take a while because Vagrant will download the box:

```
==> lamp: Loading metadata for box 'ubuntu/focal64'
    lamp: URL: https://vagrantcloud.com/ubuntu/focal64
==> lamp: Adding box 'ubuntu/focal64' (v20200409.0.0) for provider:
virtualbox
    lamp:Downloading: https://vagrantcloud.com/ubuntu/boxes/focal64/
versions/20200409.0.0/providers/virtualbox.box
    lamp: Download redirected to host: cloud-images.ubuntu.com
    lamp: Progress: 11% (Rate: 1411k/s, Estimated time remaining:
0:06:09)
```

The box is a Cloud image, but with specific configurations to run on top of Vagrant. As you can see in the logs, Vagrant is downloading the image for VirtualBox. It is also possible to provision using Hyper-V or KVM.

Vagrant Cloud (**http://vagrantcloud.com/**) is the official repository to download the images. But, of course, is not the only one. You can also create your images using Packer (**https://packer.io/**). However, if you don't, you can search there what images are available for you to create your VMs.

Figure 6.4

After the provision, if you want to check your local boxes, use the following command:

```
PS C:\Users\1511 MXTI\VagrantChapter> vagrant box list
centos/7            (virtualbox, 1801.02)
fedora/28-cloud-base (virtualbox, 20180425)
ubuntu/bionic64     (virtualbox, 20190807.0.0)
ubuntu/focal64      (virtualbox, 20200409.0.0)
ubuntu/xenial64     (virtualbox, 20180413.0.0)Status: Downloaded newer
image for
```

If you have a fresh installation, you probably have only the Ubuntu/focal64, the one we downloaded:

```
PS C:\Users\1511 MXTI\VagrantChapter> vagrant status
Current machine states:

lamp                    running (virtualbox)
docker                  running (virtualbox)
```

If everything went well with your provision, run the command `vagrant status` and it will show you the running VMs. If there is a machine that is not created yet, you can try to run the `vagrant up -provider=virtualbox` again, and see if it works. If it doesn't, check your installation and your internet connection.

Suppose, you did not define any password or SSH key to connect to these VMs, then, how do we connect to them? Vagrant is also managing that for us. With the `vagrant status,` we can see the names of the VMs and use these names to connect using the command, `vagrant ssh`:

```
PS C:\Users\1511 MXTI\VagrantChapter> vagrant ssh docker
Welcome to Ubuntu Focal Fossa (development branch) (GNU/Linux
5.4.0-21-generic x86_64)

  * Documentation:   https://help.ubuntu.com
  * Management:      https://landscape.canonical.com
  * Support:         https://ubuntu.com/advantage
```

The VM was successfully provisioned, and as you can see with the Ubuntu Focal Fossa version, Vagrant also created as user, called `vagrant`, to connect to the VMs, which has `pseudo` permission. So, we can just change the user and run all the commands:

```
vagrant@ubuntu-focal:~$ sudo su -
root@ubuntu-focal:~#
```

Now, you can manage everything as we did in the previous chapters. But, let's see how we can provision a LAMP in an automated way.

Setting up a LAMP Server

You already know the commands, and then, we can basically put the commands in the provision section of vagrant file and provision the VM again:

```
# -*- mode: ruby -*-
# vi: set ft=ruby :
```

```
Vagrant.configure("2") do |config|
  config.vm.box = "ubuntu/focal64"
  config.vm.box_check_update = false
  config.vm.provider "virtualbox" do |vb|
    vb.memory = "1024"
  end

  config.vm.define "lamp" do |lamp|
    lamp.vm.network "private_network", ip: "192.168.33.10"
    lamp.vm.hostname = "lamp"
    lamp.vm.provision "shell", inline: <<-SHELL
      sudo apt-get clean
      sudo apt update -y
      sudo apt install apache2 mysql-server php7.4 -y
    SHELL
  end

  config.vm.define "docker" do |docker|
    docker.vm.network "private_network", ip: "192.168.33.11"
    docker.vm.hostname = "docker"
    docker.vm.provision "shell", inline: <<-SHELL
      apt-get clean
      apt update -y
    SHELL
  end

  config.vm.provision "shell", inline: <<-SHELL
    apt-get clean
    apt update -y
  SHELL

end
```

In this case, I changed the `lamp.vm.provision`, including the Shell Script to install PHP, Apache, and MySQL server. Once the VM is created, run the following command:

```
PS C:\Users\1511 MXTI\VagrantChapter> vagrant provision lamp
==> lamp: Running provisioner: shell...
    lamp: Running: inline script
    lamp:
    lamp: WARNING: apt does not have a stable CLI interface. Use with
caution in scripts.
     lamp: Get:1 http://archive.ubuntu.com/ubuntu focal InRelease [265 kB]
     lamp: Hit:2 http://security.ubuntu.com/ubuntu focal-security InRelease
     lamp: Hit:3 http://archive.ubuntu.com/ubuntu focal-updates InRelease
```

You can follow the provisioning process in your Terminal. After the installation finishes, you can login into the VM:

```
PS C:\Users\1511 MXTI\VagrantChapter>vagrant ssh lamp
Welcome to Ubuntu Focal Fossa (development branch) (GNU/Linux
5.4.0-21-generic x86_64)
```

Check the services running:

```
vagrant@lamp:~$ ss -ntpl
```

State Local Address:Port Process	Recv-Q	Send-Q	Peer Address:Port
LISTEN 127.0.0.1:3306	0	151	0.0.0.0:*
LISTEN 127.0.0.53%lo:53	0	4096	0.0.0.0:*
LISTEN 0.0.0.0:22	0	128	0.0.0.0:*
LISTEN *:33060	0	70	*:*
LISTEN *:80	0	511	*:*
LISTEN [::]:22	0	128	[::]:*

Check the IP address, the one defined in the Vagrant file:

```
vagrant@lamp:~$ ip a
3: enp0s8: <BROADCAST,MULTICAST,UP,LOWER_UP> mtu 1500 qdisc fq_codel
state UP group default qlen 1000
```

```
link/ether 08:00:27:69:a5:81 brd ff:ff:ff:ff:ff:ff
inet 192.168.33.10/24 brd 192.168.33.255 scope global enp0s8
    valid_lft forever preferred_lft forever
```

You can check the IP address in the browser and see Apache running:

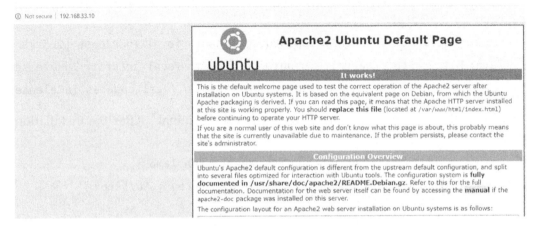

Figure 6.5

Now, every time you want to provision a new LAMP server, you can directly copy the code, or include a new VM with the provision code and it will work.

Setting up the Docker Server

This process is not different from the first one. So, let's edit the Vagrant file again:

```
# -*- mode: ruby -*-
# vi: set ft=ruby :
Vagrant.configure("2") do |config|
  config.vm.box = "ubuntu/bionic64"
  config.vm.box_check_update = false
  config.vm.provider "virtualbox" do |vb|
    vb.memory = "1024"
  end

  config.vm.define "lamp" do |lamp|
    lamp.vm.network "private_network", ip: "192.168.33.10"
    lamp.vm.hostname = "lamp"
    lamp.vm.provision "shell", inline: <<-SHELL
```

```
            sudo apt-get clean
            sudo apt update -y
            sudo apt install apache2 mysql-server php7.4 -y
        SHELL
    end

config.vm.define "docker" do |docker|
    docker.vm.box = "ubuntu/bionic64"
    docker.vm.network "private_network", ip: "192.168.33.11"
    docker.vm.hostname = "docker"
    docker.vm.provision "shell", inline: <<-SHELL
        apt clean
        apt-get update
        apt-get remove docker docker-engine docker.io containerd runc -y
        apt-get install apt-transport-https ca-certificates curl gnupg-
agent software-properties-common -y
        curl -fsSL https://download.docker.com/linux/ubuntu/gpg | apt-key
add -
        add-apt-repository "deb [arch=amd64] https://download.docker.com/
linux/ubuntu $(lsb_release -cs) stable"
        apt-get update -y
        apt-get install docker-ce docker-ce-cli containerd.io -y
    SHELL
    end

config.vm.provision "shell", inline: <<-SHELL
    apt-get clean
    apt update -y
    SHELL

end
```

Note that I changed the box just for the Docker VM because, in the Docker repo, the support for Focal Fosse was not available yet. But it is also interesting to see how we can create different VMs with different OS versions.

Now, within the provision part of the Docker VM, we have all the installation steps to setup the server. Then, you can start the machine again:

```
PS C:\Users\1511 MXTI\VagrantChapter> vagrant up docker
Bringing machine 'docker' up with 'virtualbox' provider...
==> docker: Importing base box 'ubuntu/focal64'...
==> docker: Matching MAC address for NAT networking...
==> docker: Setting the name of the VM: VagrantChapter_
docker_1586798805547_50415
==> docker: Fixed port collision for 22 => 2222. Now on port 2200.
```

Run the provision command:

```
PS C:\Users\1511 MXTI\VagrantChapter> vagrant provision docker
==> docker: Running provisioner: shell...
    docker: Running: inline script
    docker: WARNING:
    docker: apt
    docker:
    docker: does not have a stable CLI interface.
    docker: Use with caution in scripts.
    docker: Get:1 http://archive.ubuntu.com/ubuntu focal InRelease [265
kB]
```

Let's check if the installation occurred successfully:

```
PS C:\Users\1511 MXTI\VagrantChapter> vagrant ssh docker
Welcome to Ubuntu 18.04.3 LTS (GNU/Linux 4.15.0-55-generic x86_64)

  * Documentation:  https://help.ubuntu.com
  * Management:     https://landscape.canonical.com
  * Support:        https://ubuntu.com/advantageSuccessfully installed
Jinja2-2.11.1 MarkupSafe-1.1.1 Werkzeug-1.0.1 click-7.1.1 flask-1.1.1
itsdangerous-1.1.0
```

Checking that the Docker is up and running. If you face some connection issues, it is important to check if the Host Network Manager on VirtualBox is enabled:

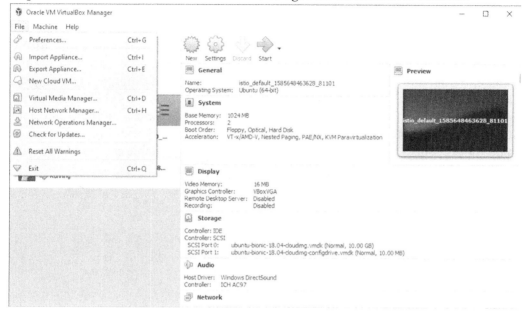

Figure 6.6

Check the column DHCP server if it is enabled, and if the IPv4 address is present in the network `192.168.33.0/24` as the following screenshot:

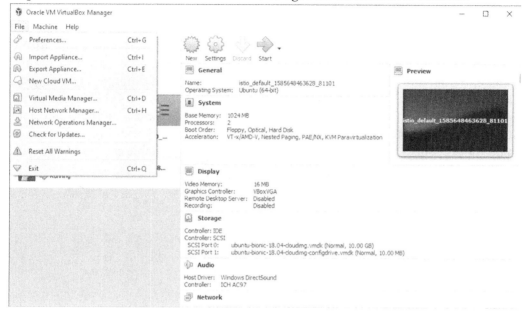

Figure 6.7

Conclusion

In this chapter, we saw the benefits of using a tool like Vagrant, which allows us to write the VM configurations like OS image, IP address, hostname, VM memory, etc. In the provision part, we could write a Shell Script and the script will run during the boot. If it doesn't, or if you want to run the script again, you can execute the command `vagrant provision`. Vagrant allows you to use different technologies, like Ansible, Puppet, or Chef to create your provision scripts. I used the Shell Script as an example, but, feel free to test and create your own scripts. Another important thing we learned is the Vagrant file. In this file, you define everything, and you can share the content with your team, so that they will be available to contribute with you to develop your environment.

CHAPTER 7
Creating Your Infrastructure Using Cloud Services

This chapter aims to introduce you to the biggest Cloud players and how we can use it to speed up the provisioning, scalability, and reliability of our Infrastructure.

Structure

In this chapter, we will discuss the following topics:

- Cloud and Main Players
- Provisioning using AWS
- Provisioning using GCP
- Provisioning using Azure

Objectives

After studying this unit, you should be able to:

- Define Cloud and how to use it
- Set up the environment on each player
- Create a simple infrastructure using the command line
- Check the infrastructure created in the Cloud console

Cloud and Main Players

Until this moment, we have been using our own computer to create everything. However, running the applications in production requires a lot of stuff, such as, high availability, backup, monitoring, redundancy, etc. In the past, many companies had their own data centers or local servers which were turned on 24*7. Hence, it takes a lot of effort to manage everything, because it is not just taking care of the virtual machines or the software; it is necessary to manage the network, storage, energy, no breaks, internet connection, and many other things that are involved in IT. Also, a team with different skills to manage everything is required to have the redundancy of people as well, because, if some employee in the company gets sick, you must have another available, in case something stops working.

When I began working in the IT industry, some of the companies that I worked for were using a service called Colocation, in which you can basically rent a Rack inside a data center, and you can install your servers. Therefore, you just need to manage your servers. The networking, energy and internet part were delegated to the company which was offering the service. After sometime, we began to use the services from a company called **SoftLayer.** They had their own data center and we could pay and use a physical server for some time when we were renting the server.

After this period, we started working with the AWS, which is a Cloud company. There, we could rent the virtual machines, exactly like the VMs that we have been created in the earlier chapters. There are a lot of benefits of using this service, such as high availability. So, if some physical server fails in their data center, you can just shut down the VM and start the VM in another server, or even pay them to do the backup for you. Thus, only one person can manage an entire infrastructure with hundreds of servers.

AWS

Amazon Web Services is currently the main Cloud player at the moment. They have dozens of services which you can use to deploy your applications, monitor, backup, create VMs, databases, queues, etc. It also allows you to create everything in an automated way using a command line, which is called **AWSCLI**. But, of course, it is not that easy to use all their services. That is why, they have created many courses and certifications, so that the people can get qualified and take the best of what their services can offer.

GCP

Google Cloud Platform is the newest one. They are offering many services like AWS, but, they still do not have all the services as theirs. Nevertheless, they have some unique services, like Big Query, which is one of the most used to query large datasets and store the data on the Cloud. Furthermore, if you are working with machine learning, they have clusters available to take the maximum performance with TensorFlow Projects. GCP is often cheaper than its other big competitors. I am using it for my personal projects.

Azure

This is the Microsoft Cloud platform. So, if you are planning to export your active directory to the Cloud, this is the one. They have unique services, like SQL server, Azure Active Directory, or even the Azure DevOps which have become very famous. Some of the big companies that I worked for in the past used Azure as their main platform, because Microsoft is a reliable company. But, they are the most expensive as well. So, if money is not your problem, and you are using Microsoft products in your applications, this is the right option.

Provisioning using AWS

AWS has its own courses to explain how to use all the services. Then, my goal here is to show you how we can provide the same infrastructure like we did using the VirtualBox and Vagrant. So, I will focus on VMs and how we can install things on it.

Therefore, your first task is to create your own AWS Account. You can visit the following link to do so:

http://console.aws.amazon.com/

After you have created your account and logged in into the console, you will see a page shown in the following figure:

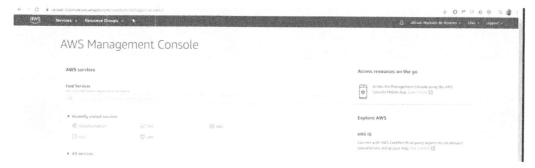

Figure 7.1

This console allows you to create any service that you want. Now, click on **Services** | **EC2** | **Running Instances**. You will see the following page:

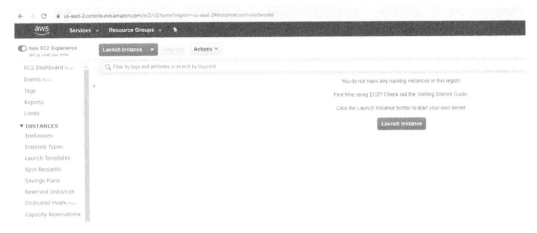

Figure 7.2

My account is empty. I have used more AWS in the past, and currently, I am using Azure in my current job, and am using GCP for personal projects. However, this is the console for you to manage your VMs. It is important for you to know where you can see your virtual machines in the console, because it is easier to see the watch you have. But starting from now, we will create everything using the command line. So, now, install Python and then write the following AWS command line:

https://www.python.org/downloads/

After Python is installed, install the AWS CLI running the following command line:

```
PS C:\Users\1511 MXTI> python -m pip install awscli --user
Collecting awscli
```

To check if the AWS CLI was installed successfully, run the following command:

```
PS C:\Users\1511 MXTI> aws --version
aws-cli/1.18.42 Python/3.8.2 Windows/10 botocore/1.15.42
```

Everything is working. Now, to configure the access, you need to create an IAM account with the programmatic access. The easiest way is by clicking on **Services** and typing IAM, like the following screenshot:

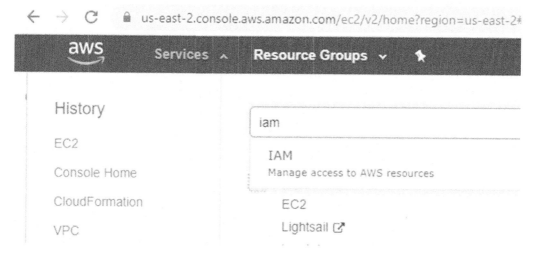

Figure 7.3

IAM means **Identity Access Management.** This service is responsible to create and manage users and groups. In the dashboard, click on **Users | Add User**:

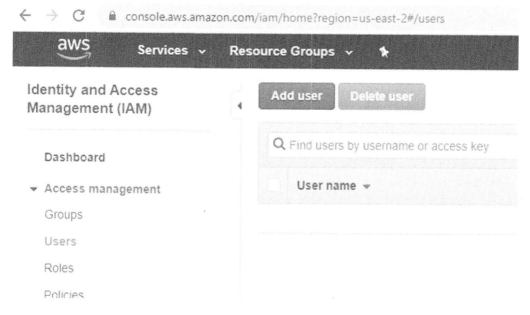

Figure 7.4

I am creating a new user, called DevOps, with the programmatic access:

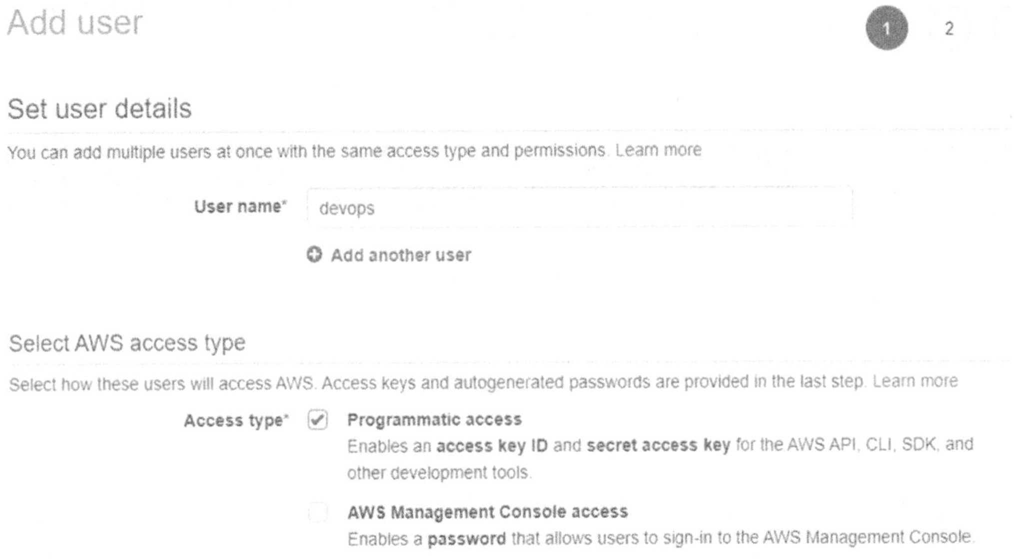

Add user

Set user details

You can add multiple users at once with the same access type and permissions. Learn more

User name*   devops

⊕ Add another user

Select AWS access type

Select how these users will access AWS. Access keys and autogenerated passwords are provided in the last step. Learn more

Access type* ☑ **Programmatic access**
Enables an **access key ID** and **secret access key** for the AWS API, CLI, SDK, and other development tools.

☐ **AWS Management Console access**
Enables a **password** that allows users to sign-in to the AWS Management Console.

Figure 7.5

Select the option **Attachexisting policies** directly and the policy **AdministratorAccess** will appear. This policy will enable our user to do everything in our AWS account. This permission is not recommended for production environments. The user must have only the permission required for a specific purpose.

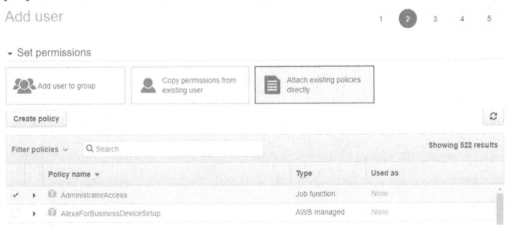

Figure 7.6

After saving your user, you will be redirected to the page with the **Access Key** and the **Secret Key**. Save these values because you will never be able to get the **Secret Key** again. The only way is creating a new user.

Figure 7.7

After following these steps, we can configure the command line and test if we are able to connect to the console. The first task is to add our keys in the local environment:

```
PS C:\Users\1511 MXTI> aws configure
AWS Access Key ID [None]: YOU_ACCESS_KEY
AWS Secret Access Key [None]: YOUR_SECRET_KEY
Default region name [None]: eu-central-1
Default output format [None]:
```

In the region name, I have set `eu-central-1`, which is respective to `Frankfurt`, because I am living in `Germany`. Often, people set this option as `us-east-1`, which is respective to Virginia in the USA. So, it is up to you.

Now, you can check if you have any example, created using the following command:

```
PS C:\Users\1511 MXTI> aws ec2 describe-instances
{
  "Reservations": []
}
```

I do not have any example, but to create one when you're using the console is an easy task. With just few clicks, you can create one. However, you cannot automate. To automate, you need to use the command line and for that, you should know every single object necessary for your VM.

The first one is creating an SSH Key. It is required to access the VM after creating it.

```
PS C:\Users\1511 MXTI> aws ec2 create-key-pair --key-name DevopsBook
--query'KeyMaterial' --output text                              YOUR_
PRIVATE_KEY
```

The parameter, `--query` was used to get only the private key in the format of a plain text. Otherwise, you can have only one string, which creates problems with the file format when you use it.

Copy the private key and save it into a file. In my case, I saved it as `devopbook.pem`, which is the standard used by AWS.

Every instance needs an IP address. Otherwise, you will not be able to access it remotely. But, to have an IP address, a subnet is required and in a sequence. Now, let's create a network using the following command:

```
PS C:\Users\1511 MXTI> aws ec2 create-vpc --cidr-block "192.168.0.0/24"
{
  "Vpc": {
    "CidrBlock": "192.168.0.0/24",
    "DhcpOptionsId": "dopt-891c21e2",
    "State": "pending",
    "VpcId": "vpc-0825b5c6f6a2a2429",
    "OwnerId": "360560397478",
    "InstanceTenancy": "default",
    "Ipv6CidrBlockAssociationSet": [],
    "CidrBlockAssociationSet": [
      {
        "AssociationId": "vpc-cidr-assoc-07b70a566b3a97801",
        "CidrBlock": "192.168.0.0/24",
        "CidrBlockState": {
          "State": "associated"
        }
      }
    ],
    "IsDefault": false,
    "Tags": []
  }
}
```

Virtual Networks on AWS are called **VPC (Virtual Private Cloud)**. I had to specify the CIDR block, which represents the network size, which allows us to have 254 available addresses. Save the VpcId. We will need it later on.

The next step is creating a subnet. Use the following command:

```
PS C:\Users\1511 MXTI> aws ec2 create-subnet --cidr-block
"192.168.0.0/24" --vpc-id vpc-0825b5c6f6a2a2429
{
  "Subnet": {
    "AvailabilityZone": "eu-central-1a",
    "AvailabilityZoneId": "euc1-az2",
    "AvailableIpAddressCount": 251,
    "CidrBlock": "192.168.0.0/24",
    "DefaultForAz": false,
    "MapPublicIpOnLaunch": false,
    "State": "pending",
    "SubnetId": "subnet-0c7889e706674e64f",
    "VpcId": "vpc-0825b5c6f6a2a2429",
    "OwnerId": "360560397478",
    "AssignIpv6AddressOnCreation": false,
    "Ipv6CidrBlockAssociationSet": [],
    "SubnetArn": "arn:aws:ec2:eu-central-1:360560397478:subnet/subnet-
0c7889e706674e64f"
  }
}
```

In the subnet too, I used the same CIDR Block. I want to have only one subnet in my VPC. But, you can create, for example, a VPC with a bigger block like /16 or /8 and split it into many subnets, as many as you want.

For security reasons, we are obligated to create security groups. It is like firewall rules, which will allow the traffic to determine the IP address, networks, and block, or allow ports depending on the protocols. Therefore, let's create it because it is a requirement, for instance:

```
PS C:\Users\1511 MXTI> aws ec2 create-security-group --group-name
devops-book  --description "Example used in the book" --vpc-id vpc-
0825b5c6f6a2a2429
{
```

```
    "GroupId": "sg-0da7b308d99365dc3"
}
```

Save the **GroupId.** Now, we need to allow all the TCP connections in this group:

```
PS C:\Users\1511 MXTI> aws ec2 authorize-security-group-ingress --group-
id sg-0da7b308d99365dc3 --protocol tcp --port 22 --cidr 0.0.0.0/0
```

For the port 22, the access can be given from any source and we can assign this SecurityGroup to any instance that we have. And finally, we can create an instance:

```
PS C:\Users\1511 MXTI> aws ec2 run-instances --count 1 --instance-type
t3.micro --key-name DevopsBook --security-group-ids sg-0da7b308d99365dc3
--subnet-id subnet-0c7889e706674e64f --image-id ami-0b418580298265d5c
{
    "Groups": [],
    "Instances": [
```

The new parameter here is the Image ID. This represents an ID of an Amazon Machine Image, which is the ISO that we used in the first chapter or the Box we used in the Vagrant chapter. To see the image options, you can give a look in the Amazon Marketplace **https://aws.amazon.com/marketplace**. I am an Ubuntu fan, so, this Image ID represents an Ubuntu version 18.04.

Check if your instance is running with the following command:

```
PS C:\Users\1511 MXTI> aws ec2 describe-instances --query
"Reservations[*].Instances[*].{Instance:InstanceId,State:State}"
[
    [
        {
            "Instance": "i-0d26f9c327b92b630",
            "State": {
                "Code": 16,
                "Name": "running"
            }
        }
    ]
]
```

If we have an instance and it is running, we are able to connect. Usually, when we create an instance using the console, a public DNS is assigned to it. Check if you have one with the following command:

```
PS C:\Users\1511 MXTI> aws ec2 describe-
instances --query "Reservations[*].Instances[*].
{Instance:InstanceId,State:State,DNS:PublicDnsName}"
[
  [
    {
      "Instance": "i-0d26f9c327b92b630",
      "State": {
        "Code": 16,
        "Name": "running"
      },
      "DNS": ""
    }
  ]
]
```

The instance does not have access to the internet. So, we need to create an Internet Gateway for that using the following command:

```
PS C:\Users\1511 MXTI>aws ec2 create-internet-gateway
{
  "InternetGateway": {
    "Attachments": [],
    "InternetGatewayId": "igw-05d94c382dd27185b",
    "Tags": []
  }
}
```

Now, we need to associate the Internet Gateway with the VPC, and all the instances inside the same VPC will have access to the internet.

```
PS C:\Users\1511 MXTI>aws ec2 attach-internet-gateway --internet-
gateway-id igw-05d94c382dd27185b --vpc-id vpc-0825b5c6f6a2a2429
```

Even creating the Internet Gateway and the VPC, it is required to create a default route. Then, all the connections, by default, will try to go through the internet first. You can check the route tables using the following command:

```
PS C:\Users\1511 MXTI>aws ec2 describe-route-tables
{
```

```
        ]
]
```

Now, we have the IP address: **18.156.153.93**assigned with the instance. We still do not have the Public DNS, but, we can try to connect using the IP. Remember the Private Key that you saved when we created the SSH? You will need it now:

PS C:\Users\1511 MXTI> **ssh -i devopskey.pem ubuntu@18.156.153.94**

The authenticity of host '18.156.153.94 (18.156.153.94)' can't be established.

ECDSA key fingerprint is SHA256:N5kMSWQKVwBLycjjUpzJ/ AsRnRbBvDVqagBJunxCXyA.

Are you sure you want to continue connecting (yes/no)? yes

Warning: Permanently added '18.156.153.94' (ECDSA) to the list of known hosts.

Welcome to Ubuntu 18.04.3 LTS (GNU/Linux 4.15.0-1057-aws x86_64)

 * Documentation: https://help.ubuntu.com

 * Management: https://landscape.canonical.com

 * Support: https://ubuntu.com/advantage

Welcome to Ubuntu 18.04.3 LTS (GNU/Linux 4.15.0-1057-aws x86_64)

 * Documentation: https://help.ubuntu.com

 * Management: https://landscape.canonical.com

 * Support: https://ubuntu.com/advantage

System information as of Tue Apr 21 19:07:47 UTC 2020

System load: 0.24   Processes: 104
Usage of /:   13.6% of 7.69GB   Users logged in: 0
Memory usage: 16%   IP address for ens5: 192.168.0.44
Swap usage: 0%

ubuntu@ip-192-168-0-44:~$

Everything is working successfully. A lot of effort is put to create something which we could do in some simple clicks using the dashboard. But, that is the life of a DevOps guy. We need to automate many using the command line, like the REST APIs, sometimes SOAP Interfaces. It does not matter what you have to automate, just do it.

If you want to delete everything, you can access the web interface directly and delete the VM. All the resources will be deleted as well.

Provisioning using GCP

Now is the time to create the same infrastructure using the Google Cloud Platform. The elements are the same in all the platforms. We will need networks, subnets, SSH keys, public IP address, etc. However, the commands and the way we are going to implement it, changes by the platform. Therefore, let's install the Google Cloud Shell and start a walkthrough of it:

https://dl.google.com/dl/cloudsdk/channels/rapid/GoogleCloudSDKInstaller.exe

To install it, double click, then click on **Next**, **Next**, and **Finish**. After the installation finishes, you need to create your configuration by running the following command:

```
PS C:\Users\1511 MXTI> gcloud config configurations create book
Created [book].
Activated [book].
```

Now, you must configure your Google account to access the platform.

```
PS C:\Users\1511 MXTI> gcloud init
Welcome! This command will take you through the configuration of gcloud.

Settings from your current configuration [book] are:
core:
disable_usage_reporting: 'True'

Pick configuration to use:
[1] Re-initialize this configuration [book] with new settings
[2] Create a new configuration
[3] Switch to and re-initialize existing configuration: [default]
Please enter your numeric choice:  1

Your current configuration has been set to: [book]

You can skip diagnostics next time by using the following flag:
gcloud init --skip-diagnostics

Network diagnostic detects and fixes local network connection issues.
Checking network connection...done.
```

```
Reachability Check passed.
Network diagnostic passed (1/1 checks passed).

Choose the account you would like to use to perform operations for
this configuration:
[1] alisson.machado@stone.com.br
[2] Log in with a new account
Please enter your numeric choice:  2

Your browser has been opened to visit:
```

I already have one existing configuration. So, I choose the re-initialize the option, and then, I add a new account, because the first email displayed is not my current Google account. This process will open a browser for you and you just need to login to your account. If everything went well with you, the terminal will show you the following message:

```
You are logged in as: [alisson.copyleft@gmail.com].

Pick cloud project to use:
[1] alisson-187813
[2] saas-205517
[3] Create a new project
Please enter numeric choice or text value (must exactly match list
item):
```

In my case, I will create a new project, called `chapter7-20200423`:

```
Please enter numeric choice or text value (must exactly match list
item):  3

Enter a Project ID. Note that a Project ID CANNOT be changed later.
Project IDs must be 6-30 characters (lowercase ASCII, digits, or
hyphens) in length and start with a lowercase letter. chapter7-20200423
Waiting for [operations/cp.8418911479956985045] to finish...done.
Your current project has been set to: [chapter7-20200423].
```

Now, my project is ready to use. To access it, go to **https://console.cloud.google.com**, click on **Projects | All** and you will see your projects there:

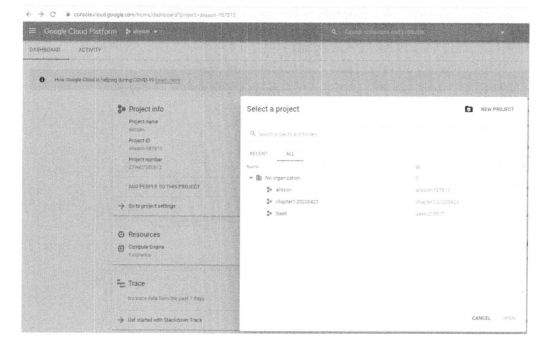

Figure 7.8

On Google, the service name to create the VMs is Google Compute Engine. Using this service, we will be able to create exactly as we did on Amazon.

Firstly, you need to activate the billing in your account. In your **Dashboard** within the project, click on `Go to Compute Engine`, and there, you have a button, called `Enable billing`, as shown in the following figure:

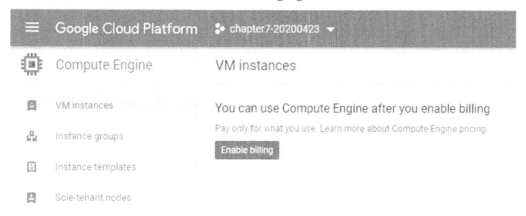

Figure 7.9

Click it and wait for a few minutes for the configuration to complete. Once the configuration is done, you can find the image with which you want to create your instance using the following command:

```
PS C:\Users\1511 MXTI>gcloud compute images list
```

NAME	PROJECT	FAMILY
DEPRECATED	STATUS	
sles-15-sp1-sap-v20200415		suse-sap-cloud
sles-15-sp1-sap	READY	
ubuntu-1604-xenial-v20200407		ubuntu-os-cloud
ubuntu-1604-lts	READY	
ubuntu-1804-bionic-v20200414		**ubuntu-os-cloud**
ubuntu-1804-lts	**READY**	
ubuntu-1910-eoan-v20200413a		ubuntu-os-cloud
ubuntu-1910	READY	
ubuntu-minimal-1604-xenial-v20200407		ubuntu-os-cloud
ubuntu-minimal-1604-lts	READY	

You will find many options. In my case, I will use `ubuntu-1804-xenial-20200407`. You also need to choose the zone where you want to create your VM:

```
PS C:\Users\1511 MXTI>gcloud compute zones list
```

NAME	REGION	STATUS	NEXT_
MAINTENANCE	TURNDOWN_DATE		
us-east1-b	**us-east1**	**UP**	
us-east1-c	us-east1	UP	
us-east1-d	us-east1	UP	

This time, I will create my VM on the US using the zone `us-east1-b`. In the AWS part, we created an instance with the `t3.micro` size. On Google, we have a respective, but with a different name:

```
PS C:\Users\1511 MXTI>gcloud compute machine-types list --zones=us-
east1-b
```

NAME	ZONE	CPUS	MEMORY_GB	DEPRECATED
e2-highmem-4	us-east1-b	4	32.00	
e2-highmem-8	us-east1-b	8	64.00	
e2-medium	us-east1-b	2	4.00	
e2-micro	**us-east1-b**	**2**	**1.00**	
e2-small	us-east1-b	2	2.00	
e2-standard-16	us-east1-b	16	64.00	

```
e2-standard-2    us-east1-b  2    8.00
e2-standard-4    us-east1-b  4    16.00
e2-standard-8    us-east1-b  8    32.00
f1-micro         us-east1-b  1    0.60
```

There are many machine family types which you can use. The difference between families is the purpose for what you want to use your VM. The E2 family was made for the general purpose VMs. So, I will use that only and the smallest size is micro, which corresponds to 2 CPUs and 1 GB of memory.

Sometimes, just setting the image name when you are creating your VM can raise an error. To avoid that, you can put the image link directly, as follows:

```
PS C:\Users\1511 MXTI> gcloud compute images list –uri
```

```
https://www.googleapis.com/compute/v1/projects/centos-cloud/global/
images/centos-6-v20200402
```

```
https://www.googleapis.com/compute/v1/projects/centos-cloud/global/
images/centos-7-v20200420
```

```
https://www.googleapis.com/compute/v1/projects/ubuntu-os-cloud/global/
images/ubuntu-1804-bionic-v20200414 https://www.googleapis.com/compute/
v1/projects/coreos-cloud/global/images/coreos-alpha-2430-0-0-v20200229
```

Therefore, the image link is as follows:

**https://www.googleapis.com/compute/v1/projects/ubuntu-os-cloud/global/
images/ubuntu-1804-bionic-v20200414**

To create your VM, run the following command:

```
PS C:\Users\1511 MXTI> gcloud compute instances create vm1 --zone=us-
east1-b --machine-type=e2-micro --image=https://www.googleapis.
com/compute/v1/projects/ubuntu-os-cloud/global/images/ubuntu-1804-
bionic-v20200414
```

```
Created [https://www.googleapis.com/compute/v1/projects/
chapter7-20200423/zones/us-east1-b/instances/vm1].
NAME  ZONE         MACHINE_TYPE  PREEMPTIBLE  INTERNAL_IP  EXTERNAL_IP
STATUS

vm1   us-east1-b   e2-micro                   10.142.0.2   35.229.97.23
RUNNING
```

The VM is now running with the external IP `25.229.97.23`. You can use it to connect to your machine. However, the Google Cloud Shell has a specific command to create the SSH key for you and automatically login into the instance:

```
PS C:\Users\1511 MXTI> gcloud compute ssh vm1
WARNING: The PuTTY PPK SSH key file for gcloud does not exist.
```

WARNING: The public SSH key file for gcloud does not exist.

WARNING: The private SSH key file for gcloud does not exist.

WARNING: You do not have an SSH key for gcloud.

WARNING: SSH keygen will be executed to generate a key.

WARNING: Invalid characters in local username [1511 MXTI]. Using username corresponding to active account: [alisson_copyleft]

No zone specified. Using zone [us-east1-b] for instance: [vm1].

Updating project ssh metadata...\Updated [https://www.googleapis.com/compute/v1/projects/chapter7-20200423].

Updating project ssh metadata...done.

Waiting for SSH key to propagate.

The server's host key is not cached in the registry. You

have no guarantee that the server is the computer you

think it is.

The server's ssh-ed25519 key fingerprint is:

ssh-ed25519 255 9c:f6:6d:58:38:8e:d7:c4:df:63:28:8b:b4:c8:53:24

If you trust this host, enter "y" to add the key to

PuTTY's cache and carry on connecting.

If you want to carry on connecting just once, without

adding the key to the cache, enter "n".

If you do not trust this host, press Return to abandon the

connection.

Store key in cache? (y/n)

Previously, you have all the output. Just to show you how it works, once the command finishes, a terminal will open for you where you have already logged in within the VM:

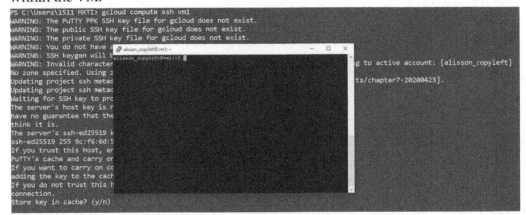

Figure 7.10

And if you want to delete your instance after learning all these steps, you need to run the following command:

```
PS C:\Users\1511 MXTI> gcloud compute instances delete vm1
No zone specified. Using zone [us-east1-b] for instance: [vm1].
The following instances will be deleted. Any attached disks configured
to be auto-deleted will be deleted unless they are attached to any
other instances or the '--keep-disks' flag is given and specifies them
for keeping. Deleting a disk is irreversible and any data on the disk
will be lost.
- [vm1] in [us-east1-b]

Do you want to continue (Y/n)?
```

For now, this is enough for you to start with your Infrastructure on GCP.

Provisioning using Azure

As we did with the other Cloud players, we are going to do the same on Azure. The goal of providing the same Infrastructure, in the same way, is to show you the process and make you feel comfortable in choosing the one you prefer.

The first step is installing the Azure command-line by the following link:

https://docs.microsoft.com/en-us/cli/azure/install-azure-cli-windows?view=azure-cli-latest

The installation process is exactly the same as all the MSI packages. Double click, click **Next**, **Next**, and **Finish**. After the installation finishes, you can run the following command to check if it is working:

```
PS C:\Users\1511 MXTI> az --version
azure-cli                      2.4.0

command-modules-nspkg          2.0.3
core                           2.4.0
nspkg                          3.0.4
telemetry                      1.0.4

Python location 'C:\Program Files (x86)\Microsoft SDKs\Azure\CLI2\
python.exe'
Extensions directory 'C:\Users\1511 MXTI\.azure\cliextensions'
```

```
Python (Windows) 3.6.6 (v3.6.6:4cf1f54eb7, Jun 27 2018, 02:47:15) [MSC
v.1900 32 bit (Intel)]
```

Now, the Azure CLI is installed successfully. To begin with, run the following command:

```
PS C:\Users\1511 MXTI> az login
```

You have logged in. Now let us find all the subscriptions to which you have access...

```
[
    {
        "cloudName": "AzureCloud",
        "isDefault": true,
        "managedByTenants": [],
        "name": "Pay-As-You-Go",
        "state": "Enabled",
        "user": {
            "name": "alisson.copyleft@gmail.com",
            "type": "user"
        }
    }
]
```

The command, az login authenticates your command line with your Azure account.

Similar to Google, where we created one project to separate all the provisioned services by context, we will do the same on Azure, but instead of creating the projects, we will create ResourceGroups.

But, before creating the ResourceGroup, we need to know which location we will use. To see the locations available, run the following command:

```
PS C:\Users\1511 MXTI>az account list-locations
[
    {
        "displayName": "Central US",
        "id": "/subscriptions/55465d5a-355d-43d1-85ce-9e518c812c0c/
        locations/centralus",
        "latitude": "41.5908",
        "longitude": "-93.6208",
```

```
        "name": "centralus",
        "subscriptionId": null
    },
    {

        "displayName": "East US",
        "id": "/subscriptions/55465d5a-355d-43d1-85ce-9e518c812c0c/
        locations/eastus",
        "latitude": "37.3719",
        "longitude": "-79.8164",
        "name": "eastus",
        "subscriptionId": null
    },
]
```

The command will show all the locations available. In my case, I will use the East US. Now, we can create ResourceGroup with the following command:

```
PS C:\Users\1511 MXTI>az group create --location eastus --name book
{
    "id": "/subscriptions/55465d5a-355d-43d1-85ce-9e518c812c0c/
    resourceGroups/book",
    "location": "eastus",
    "managedBy": null,
    "name": "book",
    "properties": {
        "provisioningState": "Succeeded"
    },
    "tags": null,
    "type": "Microsoft.Resources/resourceGroups"
}
```

Now, we have created one and called the book, and within it, we will create all the resources required for our instance. One interesting point is, when you delete your resource group, everything underlying it will be deleted as well:

```
PS C:\Users\1511 MXTI> az vm image list
```

You are viewing an offline list of images, use --all to retrieve an up-to-date list

```
[
```

```
{
    "offer": "openSUSE-Leap",
    "publisher": "SUSE",
    "sku": "42.3",
    "urn": "SUSE:openSUSE-Leap:42.3:latest",
    "urnAlias": "openSUSE-Leap",
    "version": "latest"
},
{
    "offer": "UbuntuServer",
    "publisher": "Canonical",
    "sku": "18.04-LTS",
    "urn": "Canonical:UbuntuServer:18.04-LTS:latest",
    "urnAlias": "UbuntuLTS",
    "version": "latest"
},
]
```

The preceding command will show you the images available to create your VM. As always, we will choose the UbuntuServer. Therefore, you can create the VM by running the following command:

```
PS C:\Users\1511 MXTI>az vm create -n vm1 -g book --image
Canonical:UbuntuServer:18.04-LTS:latest --admin-username ubuntu
{
    "fqdns": "",
    "id": "/subscriptions/55465d5a-355d-43d1-85ce-9e518c812c0c/
    resourceGroups/book/providers/Microsoft.Compute/virtualMachines/
    vm1",
    "location": "eastus",
    "macAddress": "00-0D-3A-9A-DF-E9",
    "powerState": "VM running",
    "privateIpAddress": "10.0.0.4",
    "publicIpAddress": "52.224.120.36",
    "resourceGroup": "book",
    "zones": ""
}
```

For the image name, we usually refer to the **URN (Uniform Resource Name)**, which is the identification for the image. The parameter, `--admin-username` is the user who will have the access to run `sudo` and do the administrative tasks.

The Azure command line is smart enough to get your default SSH-key and add it into the VM. Therefore, to connect, you can just run an SSH command as default and login:

```
PS C:\Users\1511 MXTI>ssh ubuntu@52.224.120.36
```

```
The authenticity of host '52.224.120.36 (52.224.120.36)' can't be
established.
```

```
ECDSA key fingerprint is SHA256:F/
Tb2nXVw4B3aertXLsde0wUTzNkBzu+aOwFHEFpl/A.
```

Are you sure you want to continue connecting (yes/no)? yes

```
Warning: Permanently added '52.224.120.36' (ECDSA) to the list of known
hosts.
```

```
Welcome to Ubuntu 18.04.4 LTS (GNU/Linux 5.0.0-1036-azure x86_64)Welcome
to Ubuntu 18.04.4 LTS (GNU/Linux 5.0.0-1036-azure x86_64)
```

ubuntu@vm1:~$

Now that you have everything up and running, we can delete everything to avoid some unexpected costs, except the ones we are studying:

```
PS C:\Users\1511 MXTI>az group delete --name book
```

```
Are you sure you want to perform this operation? (y/n): y
```

```
PS C:\Users\1511 MXTI>
```

You can be relieved now and be sure that everything we created before will cost.

Conclusion

I showed you how to create a VM in three of the main Cloud players. On Amazon, I showed with so much more details than the other competitors. But I do not mean that it is harder than the other. It was just my explanation. Currently, I am working with Azure. But in the past, I have worked with Amazon and Google as well. Therefore, in my view, a good DevOps engineer should be able to work with all the platforms. The concepts are same and you can deliver the same essential infrastructure. There is another concept which is called Multicloud, which aims to use all the Clouds together and you can retrieve the best from each one, like authenticating your users and services using Azure Active Directory, creating the VMs using Amazon EC2, and query your data using the Big Query on Google.

CHAPTER 8
Working with Terraform

This chapter aims to introduce you to Terraform, a tool to help you with the Multicloud concept, allowing you to create the same infrastructure among all the Cloud players in the same automated way.

Structure

In this chapter, we will discuss the following topics:

- Multicloud
- HashiCorp
- Introduction to Terraform
- Creating the Infrastructure

Objectives

After studying this unit, you should be able to:

- Know about HashiCorp tools
- Explain what Multicloud is
- Use Terraform to provide Infrastructure
- Have all your Infrastructure as Code

Multicloud

We learned in the previous chapter that there are many Cloud providers available. The most famous are AWS, GCP, and Azure. But, we also have other options like IBM Cloud, Oracle Cloud, Digital Ocean, etc. Each one of these has its services, which can be the criteria for you to decide among them. However, what can you do when you need the services from each one of them? For example, you must use an Active Directory Authentication, which is only available on Azure, but you also need BigQuery to analyze your data, and it is only available on GCP, and you also need to use the DynamoDB, which is only available on AWS. In the end, you have an on-premises infrastructure based on OpenStack. Therefore, when you need to use many Cloud providers, we call that scenario Multicloud. The challenge now is how to manage all that Infrastructure in the same way, and perhaps, by using the same tools.

HashiCorp

HashiCorp is a company that created many tools to help you with the task of managing infrastructure among different scenarios, like AWS, GCP, Azure, Digital Ocean, etc. We already have experience using their tools; Vagrant is one of the tools from HashiCorp stack which we can use for our development environments. In their stack, you can find the following tools:

- **Packer (https://www.packer.io/):** This is a tool to create your own Cloud images. In the Vagrant chapter, we used the Ubuntu Cloud image to create our VMs, but if you want to create a custom image with your application or after running a security pipeline.

- **Vagrant (https://www.vagrantup.com/):** You already know that tool. We have created many Virtual Machines and tested the applications.

- **Nomad (https://www.hashicorp.com/products/nomad/):** It is an orchestrator to deploy your applications among different environments, like the public Clouds or the private Clouds.

- **Consul (https://www.hashicorp.com/products/consul/):** It is commonly used as a Service Discovery and Service Mesh.

- **Vault (https://www.hashicorp.com/products/vault/):** It is a tool made to manage your secrets. It is an alternative for the secret services on Cloud like Azure Secret, but, of course, with some differences, like rotate the secrets automatically.

- **Terraform (https://www.hashicorp.com/products/terraform/):** It is our focus in this chapter. I will show you how to create the Infrastructure in an easy way and have the control among some code files.

Introduction to Terraform

Terraform is a tool to create and manage your Infrastructure as Code like we did using Vagrant, but here, with more details and using public Clouds with focus on productions environments, not just laboratories, as we did earlier.

You can download the open-source version by the following link:

https://www.terraform.io/downloads.html

You just need to unzip the file and include the path in the PATH environment variable. After that, you need to run the following command:

```
PS C:\Users\1511 MXTI> terraform--version

Terraform v0.12.24
```

> **If you have problems with the installation, HashiCorp has a tutorial explaining how to do it step-by-step: https://learn.hashicorp.com/tutorials/ terraform/install-cli**

The current version is v0.12.24, which is the installation of Terraform.

Now, we can create the files and create our first VM using a Cloud provider. I will do that first using the GCP which is the Cloud provider that I use for my personal projects. Then, the first step is creating a folder where you will store your code.

```
PS C:\Users\1511 MXTI> mkdirProductionInfrastructure


Directory: C:\Users\1511 MXTI


Mode                LastWriteTime         Length Name
----                -------------         ------ ----
d-----         5/10/2020   12:07 PM
ProductionInfrastructure


PS C:\Users\1511 MXTI> cd.\ProductionInfrastructure\
PS C:\Users\1511 MXTI\ProductionInfrastructure>
```

Of course, it is the best practice to split your code into many files, because it makes the code reusable and easy to manage. But in this, we will just create one virtual machine to learn the Terraform syntax and understand how it works. So, I will create everything in one single file.

To begin with, we need to create a service account which is a username and a password to create resources on my behalf. To access your Google Cloud Console (**https://console.cloud.google.com/**), go to **IAM & Admin** and on **Create service account**, create an account called terraform, as shown in the following screenshot:

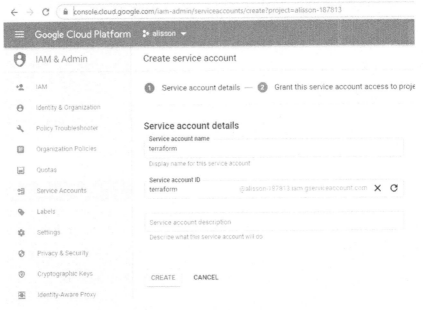

Figure 8.1

Click on **Create**, and then select the **Role Compute Admin**. This role will allow the service account to manage all the resources regarding the Compute Engine, which corresponds to our VMs.

Then, you must create a key in the JSON format as shown in the following screenshot:

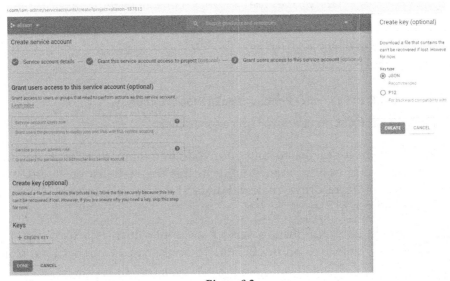

Figure 8.2

Now, you have the service account configured and ready to use with Terraform. Copy the JSON file, and put it in the same folder where we will create the Terraform code. In the folder that we created, let's create a new file, called infrastructure.tf with the following content:

```
provider "google" {
    credentials = file("terraform_sa.json")
    project     = "alisson-187813"
    region      = "us-east1"
}
```

This code is necessary for Terraform. In this file, you will use the Google providers. Providers are modules created to make the interface between your Terraform code and the platform that you want to interact with. For example, once I had a situation where I had to manage a DNS server on Linux (Bind9). When the way to do it using the Terraform was using the TSIG protocol, I had to import the DNS provider. In the case of Azure, I imported the AzureRM provider. If you want to get to know more about that, I have two posts on my personal blog.

Using Azure and Terraform: **http://alissonmachado.com.br/terraform-azure-criando-uma-infraestrutura-basica/**

Managing DNS using Terraform and TSIG: **http://alissonmachado.com.br/terraform-gerenciando-dns-com-tsig/**

Getting back to the code, the providers do not come by default with Terraform. You must download them. You can do it using the following command:

```
C:\Users\1511 MXTI\ProductionInfrastructure>   terraform init

Initializing the backend...

Initializing provider plugins...
- Checking for available provider plugins...
- Downloading plugin for provider "google" (hashicorp/google) 3.20.0...

The following providers do not have any version constraints in configuration,
so the latest version was installed.

To prevent automatic upgrades to new major versions that may contain
breaking changes, it is recommended to add version = "..." constraints to
the corresponding provider blocks in configuration, with the constraint
strings suggested below.

* provider.google: version = "~> 3.20"
```

```
Terraform has been successfully initialized!
```

You may now begin working with Terraform. Try running "terraform plan" to see any changes that are required for your infrastructure. All Terraform commands should now work.

If you ever set or change modules or backend configuration for Terraform, rerun this command to reinitialize your working directory. If you forget, other commands will detect it and remind you to do so if necessary.

Now, you are able to create the Infrastructure because you already have the provider installed in your local machine. Therefore, include the following code to create our first instance:

```
provider "google" {
    credentials = file("terraform_sa.json")
    project     = "alisson-187813"
    region      = "us-east1"
}

resource "google_compute_instance""chapter8" {
    name         = "chapter8-instance"
    machine_type = "g1-small"
    zone         = "us-east1-b"
    boot_disk {
        initialize_params {
        image = "ubuntu-1804-bionic-v20200414"
        }
    }
    network_interface {
        network      = "default"
        access_config {
        }
    }
}
```

In the preceding code, we defined that we will use a resource called `google_compute_instance` which corresponds to a VM as we did in the previous chapter. But, now we are doing so using Terraform. This instance will be created using the

Ubuntu 1804 image in the zone us-east1-b and the other details, like networking configurations. We will use the default set by Google.

The first thing when we create a new code using Terraform is to run the following command:

```
PS C:\Users\1511 MXTI\ProductionInfrastructure> terraform plan
Refreshing Terraform state in-memory prior to plan...
The refreshed state will be used to calculate this plan, but will not be
persisted to local or remote state storage.

------------------------------------------------------------------------

An execution plan has been generated and is shown below.
Resource actions are indicated with the following symbols:
  + create

Terraform will perform the following actions:

  # google_compute_instance.chapter8 will be created
  + resource "google_compute_instance" "chapter8" {
      + can_ip_forward       = false
      + cpu_platform         = (known after apply)
      + current_status       = (known after apply)
      + deletion_protection  = false
      + guest_accelerator    = (known after apply)
      + id                   = (known after apply)
      + instance_id          = (known after apply)
      + label_fingerprint    = (known after apply)
      + machine_type         = "g1-small"
      + metadata_fingerprint = (known after apply)
      + min_cpu_platform     = (known after apply)
      + name                 = "chapter8-instance"
      + project              = (known after apply)
      + self_link            = (known after apply)
      + tags_fingerprint     = (known after apply)
      + zone                 = "us-east1-b"

      + boot_disk {
```

```
        + auto_delete                  = true
        + device_name                  = (known after apply)
        + disk_encryption_key_sha256 = (known after apply)
        + kms_key_self_link           = (known after apply)
        + mode                        = "READ_WRITE"
        + source                      = (known after apply)


        + initialize_params {
            + image  = "ubuntu/ubuntu-1804-lts"
            + labels = (known after apply)
            + size   = (known after apply)
            + type   = (known after apply)
        }
    }

+ network_interface {
    + name             = (known after apply)
    + network          = "default"
    + network_ip       = (known after apply)
    + subnetwork       = (known after apply)
    + subnetwork_project = (known after apply)

    + access_config {
        + nat_ip       = (known after apply)
        + network_tier = (known after apply)
    }
}

+ scheduling {
    + automatic_restart   = (known after apply)
    + on_host_maintenance = (known after apply)
    + preemptible         = (known after apply)

    + node_affinities {
        + key       = (known after apply)
```

```
            + operator = (known after apply)

            + values   = (known after apply)

        }

    }

}
```

Plan: 1 to add, 0 to change, 0 to destroy.

Note: You didn't specify an "-out" parameter to save this plan, so Terraform can't guarantee that exactly these actions will be performed if "terraform apply" is subsequently run.

The command Terraform plan will check your project on Google and make a difference to see what is different between your code and the project on Google. In this case, we can see that everything we set will be created because of the plus signal in front of the lines (+). If some resource is going to be destroyed, you will see a minus signal (-). Also, in the last line, you will be able to see the following:

Plan: 1 to add, 0 to change, 0 to destroy.

Then you will be relieved, nothing will be destroyed. Terraform is a great tool, but you need to take care before running the commands, otherwise, you can destroy all your Infrastructure using it. There is a famous sentence about that.

If you want to make mistakes among all your production servers in an automated way, this is DevOps! Continuing with our Infrastructure, now that we are sure nothing will be deleted, we can run the command applied to create the instance:

PS C:\Users\1511 MXTI\ProductionInfrastructure> **terraform apply**

An execution plan has been generated and is shown below.

Resource actions are indicated with the following symbols:

  + create

Terraform will perform the following actions:

```
  # google_compute_instance.chapter8 will be created

  + resource "google_compute_instance" "chapter8" {

      + can_ip_forward       = false

      + cpu_platform         = (known after apply)

      + current_status       = (known after apply)

      + deletion_protection  = false
```

```
+ guest_accelerator     = (known after apply)

+ id                    = (known after apply)

+ instance_id           = (known after apply)

+ label_fingerprint     = (known after apply)

+ machine_type          = "g1-small"

+ metadata_fingerprint = (known after apply)

+ min_cpu_platform      = (known after apply)

+ name                  = "chapter8-instance"

+ project               = (known after apply)

+ self_link             = (known after apply)

+ tags_fingerprint      = (known after apply)

+ zone                  = "us-east1-b"

+ boot_disk {
    + auto_delete               = true

    + device_name               = (known after apply)

    + disk_encryption_key_sha256 = (known after apply)

    + kms_key_self_link         = (known after apply)

    + mode                      = "READ_WRITE"

    + source                    = (known after apply)

    + initialize_params {
        + image  = "ubuntu-1804-bionic-v20200414"

        + labels = (known after apply)

        + size   = (known after apply)

        + type   = (known after apply)
    }

  }

+ network_interface {
    + name              = (known after apply)

    + network           = "default"

    + network_ip        = (known after apply)

    + subnetwork        = (known after apply)

    + subnetwork_project = (known after apply)
```

```
        + access_config {
            + nat_ip        = (known after apply)
            + network_tier = (known after apply)
          }
      }

    + scheduling {
        + automatic_restart   = (known after apply)
        + on_host_maintenance = (known after apply)
        + preemptible         = (known after apply)

        + node_affinities {
            + key       = (known after apply)
            + operator = (known after apply)
            + values    = (known after apply)
          }
      }
  }
Plan: 1 to add, 0 to change, 0 to destroy.

Do you want to perform these actions?
Terraform will perform the actions described above.
Only 'yes' will be accepted to approve.

Enter a value: yes

google_compute_instance.chapter8: Creating...
google_compute_instance.chapter8: Still creating... [10s elapsed]
google_compute_instance.chapter8: Creation complete after 14s
[id=projects/alisson-187813/zones/us-east1-b/instances/chapter8-
instance]

Apply complete! Resources: 1 added, 0 changed, 0 destroyed.
```

As you can see, the command plan has already been executed when you run the command apply. To make sure that you know what will change in your infrastructure and you have to type yes, then, the instance will be created.

The instance was created successfully, but we do not have any information about the public IP address which we can use to connect to the instance. To get this information, we need to use a Terraform statement called **output**. This includes this part at the end of your current code:

```
output "name" {
    value = google_compute_instance.chapter8.name
}
output "size" {
    value = google_compute_instance.chapter8.machine_type
}
output "public_ip" {
    value = google_compute_instance.chapter8.network_interface[0].access_config[0].nat_ip
}
```

The complete file will be like this:

```
provider "google" {
    credentials = file("terraform_sa.json")
    project     = "alisson-187813"
    region      = "us-east1"
}

resource "google_compute_instance""chapter8" {
    name          = "chapter8-instance"
    machine_type = "g1-small"
    zone          = "us-east1-b"
    boot_disk {
        initialize_params {
        image = "ubuntu-1804-bionic-v20200414"
        }
    }
```

```
    network_interface {
        network      = "default"
        access_config {
            }
        }
    }

output "name" {
    value = google_compute_instance.chapter8.name
}
output "size" {
    value = google_compute_instance.chapter8.machine_type
}
output "public_ip" {
    value = google_compute_instance.chapter8.network_interface[0].
access_config[0].nat_ip
}
```

Save the file and run the `terraform plan` to check what will change:

```
PS C:\Users\1511 MXTI\ProductionInfrastructure> terraform plan
Refreshing Terraform state in-memory prior to plan...
The refreshed state will be used to calculate this plan, but will not be
persisted to local or remote state storage.

google_compute_instance.chapter8: Refreshing state... [id=projects/
alisson-187813/zones/us-east1-b/instances/chapter8-instance]

------------------------------------------------------------------

No changes. Infrastructure is up-to-date.
```

This means that Terraform did not detect any differences between your configuration and real physical resources that exist. As a result, no actions need to be performed.

The command says that we will have no changes. This is because we will not change the Infrastructure, but we will change the code to retrieve some information. Thus, you can run the command `apply`:

```
PS C:\Users\1511 MXTI\ProductionInfrastructure> terraform apply
```

```
google_compute_instance.chapter8: Refreshing state... [id=projects/
alisson-187813/zones/us-east1-b/instances/chapter8-instance]
```

```
Apply complete! Resources: 0 added, 0 changed, 0 destroyed.
```

Outputs:

```
name = chapter8-instance

public_ip = 104.196.24.122

size = g1-small
```

Nothing was changed, added, or destroyed. But, as you can see, the command brought to us the name, the `public_ip` and the instance size. If you want to see these values again, you can run `terraform output`:

```
PS C:\Users\1511 MXTI\ProductionInfrastructure> terraform output
```

```
name = chapter8-instance

public_ip = 104.196.24.122

size = g1-small
```

Even then, we cannot access the instance, because we did not define any SSH key or password. However, we can do it now, by modifying the code again:

```
resource "google_compute_instance""chapter8" {
    name          = "chapter8-instance"
    machine_type = "g1-small"
    zone          = "us-east1-b"
    boot_disk {
        initialize_params {
        image = "ubuntu-1804-bionic-v20200414"
        }
    }
    network_interface {
        network      = "default"
        access_config {
        }
    }

    metadata = {
```

```
        sshKeys = join("",["alisson:",file("id_rsa.pub")])
    }
}
```

The id_rsa.pub I copied from my default SSH key pair, which usually can be found inside the folder:

`ls ~/.ssh`

Now, the complete code is as follows:

```
provider "google" {
credentials = file("terraform_sa.json")
project      = "alisson-187813"
region       = "us-east1"
}

resource "google_compute_instance""chapter8" {
name          = "chapter8-instance"
machine_type = "g1-small"
zone          = "us-east1-b"
boot_disk {
initialize_params {
image = "ubuntu-1804-bionic-v20200414"
}
}
network_interface {
network       = "default"
access_config {
}
}

metadata = {
sshKeys = join("",["alisson:",file("id_rsa.pub")])
}
}

output "name" {
```

```
    value = google_compute_instance.chapter8.name
}
output "size" {
    value = google_compute_instance.chapter8.machine_type
}
output "public_ip" {
    value = google_compute_instance.chapter8.network_interface[0].
access_config[0].nat_ip
}
```

As long as we are including more things in our code, Terraform is getting more and more interesting. Let's run the `terraform plan` to see what the new changes are:

```
PS C:\Users\1511 MXTI\ProductionInfrastructure> terraform plan
Refreshing Terraform state in-memory prior to plan...
The refreshed state will be used to calculate this plan, but will not be
persisted to local or remote state storage.

google_compute_instance.chapter8: Refreshing state... [id=projects/
alisson-187813/zones/us-east1-b/instances/chapter8-instance]

------------------------------------------------------------------------

An execution plan has been generated and is shown below.
Resource actions are indicated with the following symbols:
  ~ update in-place

Terraform will perform the following actions:

  # google_compute_instance.chapter8 will be updated in-place
  ~ resource "google_compute_instance" "chapter8" {
        can_ip_forward       = false
        cpu_platform         = "Intel Haswell"
        current_status       = "RUNNING"
        deletion_protection  = false
        enable_display       = false
        guest_accelerator    = []
        id                   = "projects/alisson-187813/zones/us-
east1-b/instances/chapter8-instance"
```

```
        instance_id            = "9170008912891805003"
        label_fingerprint    = "42WmSpB8rSM="
        labels                 = {}
        machine_type         = "g1-small"
    ~ metadata               = {
          + "sshKeys" = <<~EOT
                alisson:ssh-rsa
AAAAB3NzaC1yc2EAAAADAQABAAABAQChi8HX26xv9Rk9gz47Qhb+Tu7MRqGIyPxnheIeEg
Fad/dlqG4w4pY7y5dtx5LNGE9C01varco5dZagqsHplI7M+5ECSvjAuS6b5rkYZwZiZru
DXxckcQHFpr2yIz3DOzKRTUc5Hg5JHF5aymiqyVfTsxL/aI/LDY8Ikh+INn3S9+b5
bZtU+74tA6y uqth5SCtNSWwMUlv7QL6ONHtQiviAjBe+ksDBBV6thWz2ZIJA/
jApSIBJWK9AWmZwq2hFy9sOZArUDB2Kt 6kl3rIZnHpqJ/GMUCxFhtggYamJ5J2H62
77qLFqLZ/8tum9uc5l/lSWYKTDm2+E/prQfmFrxPf9 alisson

            EOT
        }
        metadata_fingerprint = "bxkbv_NPHas="
        name                 = "chapter8-instance"
        project              = "alisson-187813"
        resource_policies    = []
        self_link            = "https://www.googleapis.com/compute/v1/
projects/alisson-187813/zones/us-east1-b/instances/chapter8-instance"
        tags                 = []
        tags_fingerprint     = "42WmSpB8rSM="
        zone                 = "us-east1-b"

        boot_disk {
            auto_delete = true
            device_name = "persistent-disk-0"
            mode        = "READ_WRITE"
            source      = "https://www.googleapis.com/compute/v1/
projects/alisson-187813/zones/us-east1-b/disks/chapter8-instance"

            initialize_params {
                image = "https://www.googleapis.com/compute/v1/
projects/ubuntu-os-cloud/global/images/ubuntu-1804-bionic-v20200414"
                labels = {}
                size   = 10
                type   = "pd-standard"
```

```
                }
        }

        network_interface {
                name                = "nic0"
                network             = "https://www.googleapis.com/compute/v1/
projects/alisson-187813/global/networks/default"
                network_ip          = "10.142.0.3"
                subnetwork          = "https://www.googleapis.com/compute/v1/
projects/alisson-187813/regions/us-east1/subnetworks/default"
                subnetwork_project = "alisson-187813"

                access_config {
                    nat_ip       = "104.196.24.122"
                    network_tier = "PREMIUM"
                }
        }

        scheduling {
            automatic_restart   = true
            on_host_maintenance = "MIGRATE"
            preemptible         = false
        }

        shielded_instance_config {
            enable_integrity_monitoring = true
            enable_secure_boot          = false
            enable_vtpm                 = true
        }
    }
Plan: 0 to add, 1 to change, 0 to destroy.

-----------------------------------------------------------------------
```

Note: You didn't specify an "-out" parameter to save this plan, so Terraform can't guarantee that exactly these actions will be performed if "terraform apply" is subsequently run.

Finally, we can see the first change. Since the SSH Keys are stored in the instance metadata, when we have an existing resource and we want to modify, the filed change is increased.

```
Plan: 0 to add, 1 to change, 0 to destroy.
```

So, one thing changed and nothing was destroyed. This is important. Thus, we can run the `terraform apply`:

```
PS C:\Users\1511 MXTI\ProductionInfrastructure> terraform apply

google_compute_instance.chapter8: Refreshing state... [id=projects/
alisson-187813/zones/us-east1-b/instances/chapter8-instance]

An execution plan has been generated and is shown below.

Resource actions are indicated with the following symbols:

  ~ update in-place

Terraform will perform the following actions:

  # google_compute_instance.chapter8 will be updated in-place
  ~ resource "google_compute_instance" "chapter8" {
        can_ip_forward        = false
        cpu_platform          = "Intel Haswell"
        current_status        = "RUNNING"
        deletion_protection   = false
        enable_display        = false
        guest_accelerator     = []
        id                    = "projects/alisson-187813/zones/us-eas
t1-b/instances/chapter8-instance"
        instance_id           = "9170008912891805003"
        label_fingerprint     = "42WmSpB8rSM="
        labels                = {}
        machine_type          = "g1-small"
      ~ metadata              = {
          + "sshKeys" = <<~EOT
                alisson:ssh-rsa
AAAAB3NzaC1yc2EAAAADAQABAAABAQChi8HX26xv9Rk9gz47Qhb+Tu7MRqGIyPx
nheIeEgFad/dlqG4w4pY7y5dtx5LNGE9C01varco5dZa gqsHplI7M+5ECSvjAuS6
b5rkYZwZiZruDXx ckcQHFpr2yIz3DOzKRTUc5Hg5JHF5aymiqyVfTsxL/aI/
LDY8Ikh+INn3S9+b5bZtU+74tA6yuqth5SCtNSW wMUlv7QL6ONHtQiviAjBe+ksD
```

BBV6thWz2ZIJA/jApSIBJWK9AWmZwq2hFy9sOZArUDB2Kt6kl3rIZnHpqJ/
GMUCxFhtggYamJ5J2H6277qLFqLZ/8 tum9uc5l/1SWYKTDm2+E/prQfmFrxPf9 alisson

```
            EOT
        }
        metadata_fingerprint = "bxkbv_NPHas="
        name                 = "chapter8-instance"
        project              = "alisson-187813"
        resource_policies    = []
        self_link            = "https://www.googleapis.com/compute/v1/
projects/alisson-187813/zones/us-east1-b/instances/chapter8-instance"
        tags                 = []
        tags_fingerprint     = "42WmSpB8rSM="
        zone                 = "us-east1-b"

        boot_disk {
            auto_delete = true
            device_name = "persistent-disk-0"
            mode        = "READ_WRITE"
            source      = "https://www.googleapis.com/compute/v1/
projects/alisson-187813/zones/us-east1-b/disks/chapter8-instance"

            initialize_params {
                image  = "https://www.googleapis.com/compute/v1/
projects/ubuntu-os-cloud/global/images/ubuntu-1804-bionic-v20200414"
                labels = {}
                size   = 10
                type   = "pd-standard"
            }
        }

        network_interface {
            name        = "nic0"
            network     = "https://www.googleapis.com/compute/v1/
projects/alisson-187813/global/networks/default"
            network_ip  = "10.142.0.3"
            subnetwork  = "https://www.googleapis.com/compute/v1/
projects/alisson-187813/regions/us-east1/subnetworks/default"
```

```
            subnetwork_project = "alisson-187813"

            access_config {
                nat_ip       = "104.196.24.122"
                network_tier = "PREMIUM"
            }
        }

        scheduling {
            automatic_restart   = true
            on_host_maintenance = "MIGRATE"
            preemptible         = false
        }

        shielded_instance_config {
            enable_integrity_monitoring = true
            enable_secure_boot          = false
            enable_vtpm                 = true
        }
    }
```

Plan: 0 to add, 1 to change, 0 to destroy.

Do you want to perform these actions?
Terraform will perform the actions described above.
Only 'yes' will be accepted to approve.

Enter a value: yes

google_compute_instance.chapter8: Modifying... [id=projects/
alisson-187813/zones/us-east1-b/instances/chapter8-instance]
google_compute_instance.chapter8: Still modifying... [id=projects/
alisson-187813/zones/us-east1-b/instances/chapter8-instance, 10s
elapsed]
google_compute_instance.chapter8: Modifications complete after 13s
[id=projects/alisson-187813/zones/us-east1-b/instances/chapter8-
instance]

Apply complete! Resources: 0 added, 1 changed, 0 destroyed.

Outputs:

```
name = chapter8-instance

public_ip = 104.196.24.122

size = g1-small
```

The changes were applied successfully, and then, we can test if the access is working properly:

```
PS C:\Users\1511 MXTI\ProductionInfrastructure>ssh
alisson@104.196.24.122

Welcome to Ubuntu 18.04.4 LTS (GNU/Linux 5.0.0-1034-gcp x86_64)

* Documentation:  https://help.ubuntu.com

* Management:     https://landscape.canonical.com

* Support:        https://ubuntu.com/advantage

System information as of Mon May 11 13:21:39 UTC 2020

System load:  0.0            Processes:          94

Usage of /:   12.8% of 9.52GB  Users logged in:    0

Memory usage: 13%            IP address for ens4: 10.142.0.3

Swap usage:   0%

* Ubuntu 20.04 LTS is out, raising the bar on performance, security,
and optimization for Intel, AMD, Nvidia, ARM64, and Z15 as well as
AWS, Azure, and Google Cloud.

https://ubuntu.com/blog/ubuntu-20-04-lts-arrives

0 packages can be updated.
0 updates are security updates.

The programs included with the Ubuntu system are free software; the exact
distribution terms for each program are described in the individual files
in /usr/share/doc/*/copyright.

Ubuntu comes with ABSOLUTELY NO WARRANTY, to the extent permitted by
applicable law.

alisson@chapter8-instance:~$
```

It works! Perfect! We created everything, just managing some lines of code, and now we have an instance up and running, just accessing the console to create the service account. As a final step, I think we can destroy everything using the command terraform destroy and see how it works:

```
PS C:\Users\1511 MXTI\ProductionInfrastructure>terraform destroy
google_compute_instance.chapter8: Refreshing state... [id=projects/
alisson-187813/zones/us-east1-b/instances/chapter8-instance]

An execution plan has been generated and is shown below.
Resource actions are indicated with the following symbols:
  - destroy

Terraform will perform the following actions:

  # google_compute_instance.chapter8 will be destroyed
  - resource "google_compute_instance" "chapter8" {
      - can_ip_forward        = false -> null
      - cpu_platform          = "Intel Haswell" -> null
      - current_status        = "RUNNING" -> null
      - deletion_protection   = false -> null
      - enable_display        = false -> null
      - guest_accelerator     = [] -> null
      - id                    = "projects/alisson-187813/zones/us-
east1-b/instances/chapter8-instance" -> null
      - instance_id           = "9170008912891805003" -> null
      - label_fingerprint     = "42WmSpB8rSM=" -> null
      - labels                = {} -> null
      - machine_type          = "g1-small" -> null
      - metadata              = {
          - "sshKeys" = <<~EOT
                alisson:ssh-rsa AAAAB3NzaC1yc2EAAAADAQABAAABAQChi8HX2
6xv9Rk9gz47Qhb+Tu7MRqGIyPxnheIeEgFad/
dlqG4w4p Y7y5dtx 5LNGE9C01varco5dZagqsHplI7M
+5ECSvjAuS6b5rkYZwZiZruDXxckcQHFpr2yIz3DOzKRTUc5Hg5JHF5aymiqyVfTsxL/
aI/LDY8Ikh+INn3S9+b5bZtU+74tA6yuqth5SCtNSWwMUlv7QL6ONHtQiviAj
Be+ksDBBV6thWz2ZIJA/jApSIBJWK9AWmZwq2hFy9sOZArUDB2Kt6k13rIZnHpqJ /
GMUCxFhtggYamJ5J2H6277qLFqLZ/8tum9uc5l/lSWYKTDm2+E/prQfmFrxPf9 alisson
                EOT
        } -> null
```

```
        - metadata_fingerprint = "1ZHcUBfXG-4=" -> null

        - name                  = "chapter8-instance" -> null

        - project               = "alisson-187813" -> null

        - resource_policies     = [] -> null

        - self_link             = "https://www.googleapis.com/compute/v1/
projects/alisson-187813/zones/us-east1-b/instances/chapter8-instance" ->
null

        - tags                  = [] -> null

        - tags_fingerprint      = "42WmSpB8rSM=" -> null

        - zone                  = "us-east1-b" -> null


        - boot_disk {
            - auto_delete = true -> null

            - device_name = "persistent-disk-0" -> null

            - mode        = "READ_WRITE" -> null

            - source      = "https://www.googleapis.com/compute/v1/projects/
alisson-187813/zones/us-east1-b/disks/chapter8-instance" -> null

            - initialize_params {
                - image = "https://www.googleapis.com/compute/v1/projects/
ubuntu-os-cloud/global/images/ubuntu-1804-bionic-v20200414" -> null

                - labels = {} -> null

                - size   = 10 -> null

                - type   = "pd-standard" -> null

            }

        }

        - network_interface {
            - name              = "nic0" -> null

            - network           = "https://www.googleapis.com/compute/v1/
projects/alisson-187813/global/networks/default" -> null

            - network_ip        = "10.142.0.3" -> null

            - subnetwork        = "https://www.googleapis.com/compute/v1/
projects/alisson-187813/regions/us-east1/subnetworks/default" -> null

            - subnetwork_project = "alisson-187813" -> null

            - access_config {
```

```
            - nat_ip        = "104.196.24.122" -> null
            - network_tier = "PREMIUM" -> null
          }
        }

      - scheduling {
          - automatic_restart   = true -> null
          - on_host_maintenance = "MIGRATE" -> null
          - preemptible         = false -> null
        }

      - shielded_instance_config {
          - enable_integrity_monitoring = true -> null
          - enable_secure_boot          = false -> null
          - enable_vtpm                 = true -> null
        }
    }
Plan: 0 to add, 0 to change, 1 to destroy.

Do you really want to destroy all resources?
Terraform will destroy all your managed infrastructure, as shown above.
There is no undo. Only 'yes' will be accepted to confirm.

Enter a value: yes

google_compute_instance.chapter8: Destroying... [id=projects/
alisson-187813/zones/us-east1-b/instances/chapter8-instance]
google_compute_instance.chapter8: Still destroying... [id=projects/
alisson-187813/zones/us-east1-b/instances/chapter8-instance, 10s elapsed]
google_compute_instance.chapter8: Still destroying... [id=projects/
alisson-187813/zones/us-east1-b/instances/chapter8-instance, 20s elapsed]
google_compute_instance.chapter8: Still destroying... [id=projects/
alisson-187813/zones/us-east1-b/instances/chapter8-instance, 30s elapsed]
google_compute_instance.chapter8: Still destroying... [id=projects/
alisson-187813/zones/us-east1-b/instances/chapter8-instance, 40s elapsed]
google_compute_instance.chapter8: Still destroying... [id=projects/
alisson-187813/zones/us-east1-b/instances/chapter8-instance, 50s elapsed]
```

```
google_compute_instance.chapter8: Still destroying... [id=projects/
alisson-187813/zones/us-east1-b/instances/chapter8-instance, 1m0s elapsed]

google_compute_instance.chapter8: Still destroying... [id=projects/
alisson-187813/zones/us-east1-b/instances/chapter8-instance, 1m10s elapsed]

google_compute_instance.chapter8: Still destroying... [id=projects/
alisson-187813/zones/us-east1-b/instances/chapter8-instance, 1m20s elapsed]

google_compute_instance.chapter8: Still destroying... [id=projects/
alisson-187813/zones/us-east1-b/instances/chapter8-instance, 1m30s elapsed]

google_compute_instance.chapter8: Still destroying... [id=projects/
alisson-187813/zones/us-east1-b/instances/chapter8-instance, 1m40s elapsed]

google_compute_instance.chapter8: Still destroying... [id=projects/
alisson-187813/zones/us-east1-b/instances/chapter8-instance, 1m50s elapsed]

google_compute_instance.chapter8: Still destroying... [id=projects/
alisson-187813/zones/us-east1-b/instances/chapter8-instance, 2m0s elapsed]

google_compute_instance.chapter8: Still destroying... [id=projects/
alisson-187813/zones/us-east1-b/instances/chapter8-instance, 2m10s elapsed]

google_compute_instance.chapter8: Destruction complete after 2m19s

Destroy complete! Resources: 1 destroyed.
```

Perfect! Now, we do not have anything else costing in our GCP account and if you want to create the Infrastructure again, you can just run the command `terraform apply`. But, with this name you will have the output with the IP address and the SSH key already configured in one shot. If you want to create more instances, just copy and paste the code changing the instance name. The SSH key can be the same for all the instances.

Conclusion

This chapter showed us that it is not necessary to learn the command line of all the Cloud players or even install the SDK for each one of them. Using Terraform, we are able to code the Infrastructure using the Terraform syntax, change the providers to make different integrations, and see what will be changed, created, or destroyed. I really recommend you to explore other providers to integrate with Azure, AWS, Digital Ocean, and play around other providers which are not related to the Cloud player, but they can help you to provide Infrastructure, like the DNS module.

CHAPTER 9
Working with Git

This chapter aims to introduce you to Git, a tool to help you work in the same code, and collaborate with other developers in the same project in a remote way.

Structure

In this chapter, we will discuss the following topics:

- Git
- GitFlow
- GitHub

Objectives

After studying this unit, you should be able to:

- Install and use Git with the local repositories
- Understand the GitFlow and how it can be applied in the daily work
- Share your code with other people using GitHub

Git

Git is a tool created by *Linus Torvalds*, the creator of the Linux system. The tool was created to help the Linux developers control the development flow among many developers around the world. It helps to solve conflicts, track the modifications, or even revert the configurations that were working before and stopped working in a new version.

To install Git, you can access the following link:

https://git-scm.com/download/win

The installation process is the same that we did for all Windows applications; just **Next**, **Next**, and **Finish**. After the installation, you will find a new program called **Git Bash**, which allows you to create your local repos and use the Git commands to create versions of your application:

Figure 9.1

In the next steps, I will show you some basic commands which are enough for you to use Git in your daily work. Of course, it is possible to create an entire book just to explain the Git commands and how to deal with conflicts and different strategies of versioning code. However, let's keep with the basics because "done is better than perfect":

```
1511 MXTI@avell MINGW64 ~
$ mkdir Chapter09

1511 MXTI@avell MINGW64 ~
$ cd Chapter09/
```

Aforementioned, you have the output of my Git Bash. Creating a folder, called `Chapter09` and get inside that folder. Here, I will create my first repository:

```
1511 MXTI@avell MINGW64 ~/Chapter09
$ git init
Initialized empty Git repository in C:/Users/1511 MXTI/Chapter09/.git/
```

The command `git init` is responsible to initialize any folder of a Git repository. It basically creates a folder, called `.git` with a pre-defined folder structure which will store the files with the metadata for your code, like what was changed from the current version of the code and your modifications, which files you want to send to the new version, and other things. A repository is a folder where you store and track the modifications of your code.

Now, we can use any text editor to create some code and track the changes. I will use the Visual Studio Code, because it is my favorite. But, feel free to use any according to your preference:

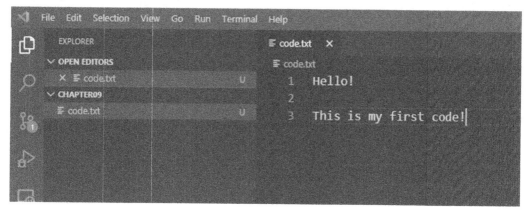

Figure 9.2

I created a new file called `code.txt` in the text editor, just too as an example with some random content. Within the Git repositories, we can track the modifications of any kind of the text file, Python codes, C++ codes, Java, or whatsoever.

The next step is to check what changed since the beginning when I created the repository and created the file, the Visual Studio Code as integration with the PowerShell. Thus, I will use it to run the Git commands.

The first command is `git status`:

```
PS C:\Users\1511 MXTI\Chapter09> git status
On branch master

No commits yet
```

```
Untracked files:
(use "git add <file>..." to include in what will be committed)
code.txt

nothing added to commit but untracked files present (use "git add" to
track)
```

In the preceding command, we can see that we are on the branch master and we have one untraced file, called `code.txt`. The branches are the versions that you can have of the same project. You can use it in the way that you want, with the name that you want. However, create a flow which helps you to keep a standard of the organization. Otherwise, each project would have a versioning strategy.

GitFlow

Now, when we start working on a project, we have the code files that are already in production, and we cannot work in the main branch, because of the CI/CD pipelines. We need to generate a new version of our software with the complete code.

Let's commit the first version of the code, which will be shared among all the developers working in the same project:

```
PS C:\Users\1511 MXTI\Chapter09> git add --all
PS C:\Users\1511 MXTI\Chapter09> git commit -m "uploading the scaffold
of the project"
[master (root-commit) f6284bf] uploading the scaffold of the project
1 file changed, 3 insertions(+)
create mode 100644 code.txt
```

If we run the `git status` again, nothing is untraced or pending to commit:

```
PS C:\Users\1511 MXTI\Chapter09> git status
On branch master
nothing to commit, working tree clean
```

To check the branches you have, run the following command:

```
PS C:\Users\1511 MXTI\Chapter09> git branch
* master
```

Now, we need to work on that code without breaking the version in production, which corresponds to the branch master. Then, we will create a new branch, called `develop`, which is the branch respective to a new version of our software:

```
PS C:\Users\1511 MXTI\Chapter09> git checkout -b develop
Switched to a new branch 'develop'
```

We created a new branch. Now, if we run the command git branch again, we can see that another version of our current code is created, which we can modify without changing anything in the current version:

```
S C:\Users\1511 MXTI\Chapter09> git branch
* develop
master
```

We created a new branch, then if we run the command **git branch** again, we can see that another version of our current code was created, which we can modify without changing anything in the current version:

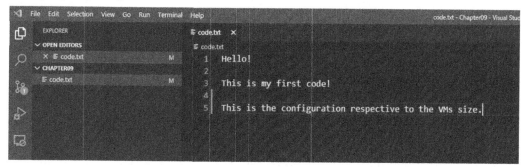

Figure 9.3

In the preceding figure, I have added a new line into our code. This book is about infrastructure. Therefore, I want to show that we can include the new code respective to infrastructure, and we also have the development infrastructure and the production infrastructure, whichever one has their configurations and codes.

I can run the command git status again, and see what has changed:

```
PS C:\Users\1511 MXTI\Chapter09> git status
On branch develop
Changes not staged for commit:
(use "git add <file>..." to update what will be committed)
(use "git restore <file>..." to discard changes in working directory)
modified:   code.txt

no changes added to commit (use "git add" and/or "git commit -a")
```

Different from the first file, the `code.txt` is now modified, not untraced as we saw in the first command, which means that it is not a new file and the file was modified. If you want to check what has changed from the old version, you can use the following command:

```
PS C:\Users\1511 MXTI\Chapter09> git diff code.txt

diff --git a/code.txt b/code.txt

index 70274ce..9c5fd1c 100644

--- a/code.txt

+++ b/code.txt

@@ -1,3 +1,5 @@

Hello!

-This is my first code!
\ No newline at end of file

+This is my first code!

+

+This is the configuration respective to the VMs size.
\ No newline at end of file
```

Here, we can see the differences between the two versions. Where we have the (+) plus sign, means that the lines were included in the file, with the (-)minus sign, we have what was removed from the old version. To save this new version and share with the other developers, we must add the file in this new version and commit the changes:

```
PS C:\Users\1511 MXTI\Chapter09> git add --all

PS C:\Users\1511 MXTI\Chapter09> git commit -m "adding new configurations"

[develop 806990f] adding new configurations

1 file changed, 3 insertions(+), 1 deletion(-)
```

Now, let's assume that we tested everything and we want to put the development version in production. Now, we need to merge the development code with the production code. To do this, we can use the following command:

```
PS C:\Users\1511 MXTI\Chapter09> git checkout master

Switched to branch 'master'

PS C:\Users\1511 MXTI\Chapter09> git merge develop

Updating f6284bf..806990f
```

```
Fast-forward
code.txt | 4 +++-
1 file changed, 3 insertions(+), 1 deletion(-)
```

Perfect! Now we have the development version in production. So, we can deploy it and start to work again in the other version. But, let's make the things a little bit more sophisticated. Firstly, we have to go back to the development branch:

```
PS C:\Users\1511 MXTI\Chapter09>git checkout develop
Switched to branch 'develop'
```

We can suppose that we want to change the current operating system of the infrastructure. Assuming that it is based on CentOS, we want to change to Ubuntu. However, we cannot change it in the development environment, because it can stop the developers working on their own projects. Therefore, I have to create a new branch based on the development branch which we usually call the feature branch.

```
PS C:\Users\1511 MXTI\Chapter09>git checkout -b feature-ubuntu
Switched to a new branch 'feature-ubuntu'
```

Now, I will write the new code:

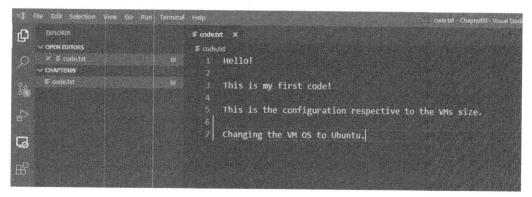

Figure 9.4

After testing the code in the ephemeral environment which was created based on the development environment and making sure that it is working, we can commit the changes and merge it with the development environment:

```
PS C:\Users\1511 MXTI\Chapter09> git add --all
PS C:\Users\1511 MXTI\Chapter09> git commit -m "changing the os"
[feature-ubuntu 5b4ce7a] changing the os
1 file changed, 3 insertions(+), 1 deletion(-)
```

Now, we can change from the feature branch to the development branch and merge the code:

```
PS C:\Users\1511 MXTI\Chapter09> git checkout develop
Switched to branch 'develop'
PS C:\Users\1511 MXTI\Chapter09> git merge feature-ubuntu
Updating 806990f..5b4ce7a
Fast-forward
code.txt | 4 +++-
1 file changed, 3 insertions(+), 1 deletion(-)
```

The code was merged successfully and now assuming that we have tested it in the development environment and everything worked seamlessly, it is time to merge with the production environment:

```
PS C:\Users\1511 MXTI\Chapter09> git checkout master
Switched to branch 'master'
PS C:\Users\1511 MXTI\Chapter09> git merge develop
Updating 806990f..5b4ce7a
Fast-forward
code.txt | 4 +++-
1 file changed, 3 insertions(+), 1 deletion(-)
```

GitHub

The commands ran in the local machine and in a local environment. It was just the basic steps, but I am pretty sure that with these commands you will be able to do 80% of your work every day. If you cannot, there are many tools to help you with the Git commands, like `git kraken`, or you can even use plugins for Visual Studio Code. We need to have in mind that as bigger as your team is, you will have more conflicts and more changes happening at the same time.

To share our code, we can use many tools, like GitLab, GitHub, Bitbucket. There are dozens of services to help you with it. Let's use the GitHub because it is the most famous. But, for some of my personal projects, I use the Bitbucket, because we can have unlimited private repos.

You can create your own GitHub account for free on their website:

https://github.com/

After creating your account, you will be able to create your first repository, as I am doing in the following screenshot:

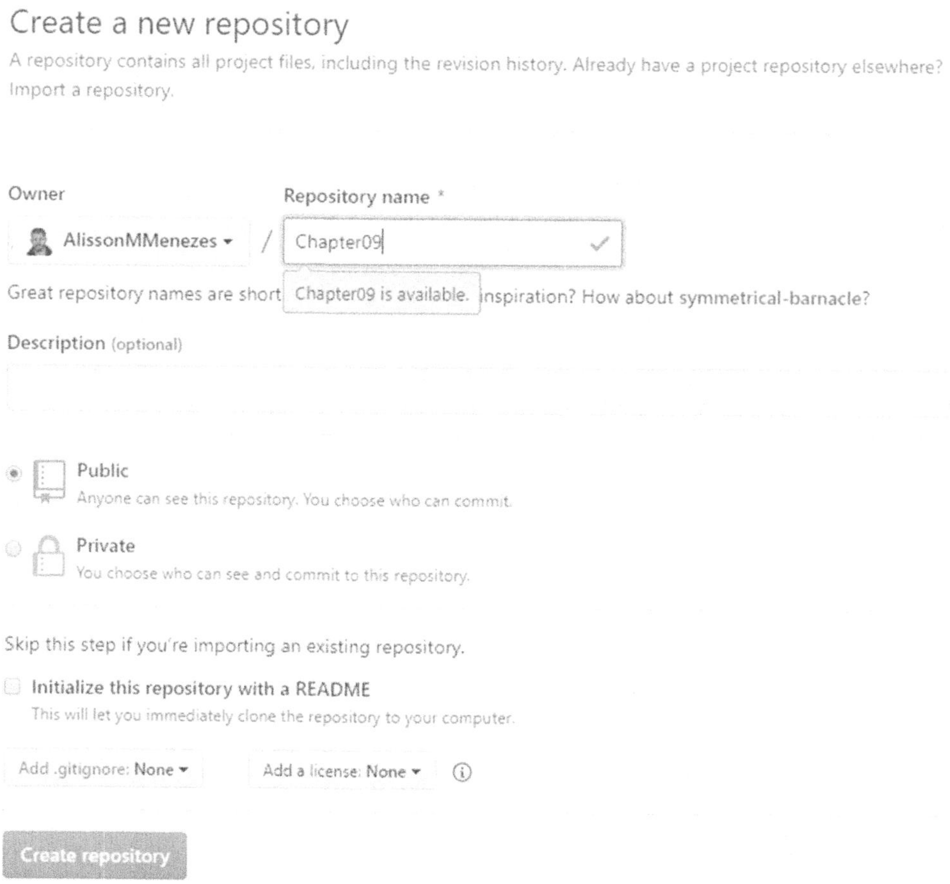

Create a new repository

A repository contains all project files, including the revision history. Already have a project repository elsewhere? Import a repository.

Owner   Repository name *

👤 AlissonMMenezes ▾   / | Chapter09| ✓ |

Great repository names are short | Chapter09 is available. | nspiration? How about symmetrical-barnacle?

Description (optional)

| |

⦿ 📘 Public
    Anyone can see this repository. You choose who can commit.

◯ 🔒 Private
    You choose who can see and commit to this repository.

Skip this step if you're importing an existing repository.

☐ Initialize this repository with a README
    This will let you immediately clone the repository to your computer.

| Add .gitignore: None ▾ | | Add a license: None ▾ | ⓘ

| Create repository |

Figure 9.5

After creating the repository, the initial page will show some commands in case you have an existing repo and you want to upload it, or if you want to clone the empty repository. In our case, we already have the code with some commits and we want to send it to Git.

The next screenshot will show the initial page. But the most important information is the following one:

https://github.com/AlissonMMenezes/Chapter09.git

Which corresponds to the address of our remote repository:

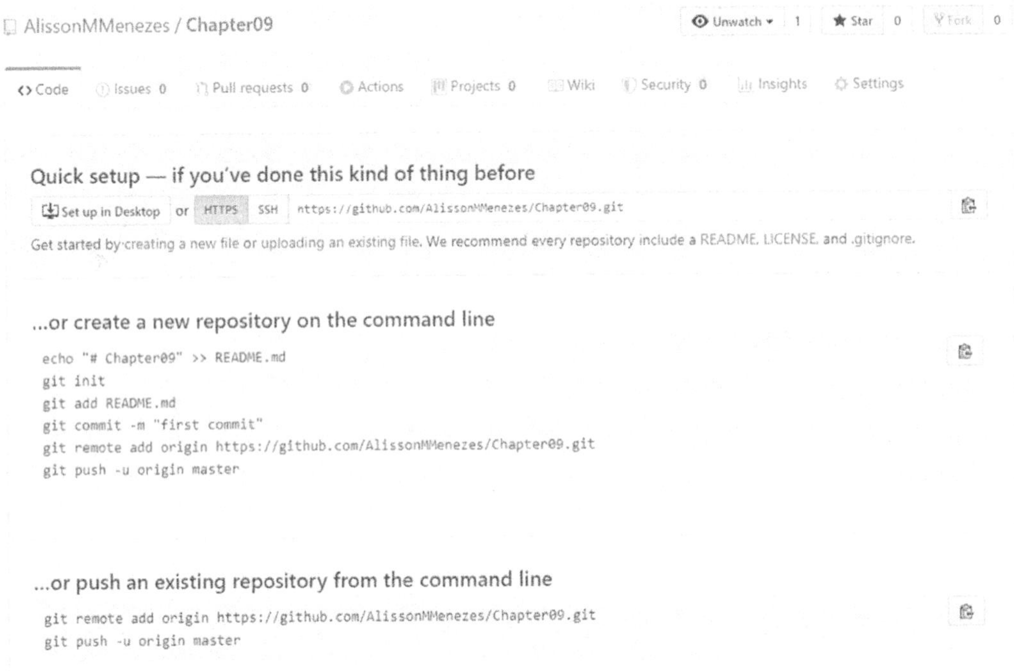

AlissonMMenezes / Chapter09

```
echo "# Chapter09" >> README.md
git init
git add README.md
git commit -m "first commit"
git remote add origin https://github.com/AlissonMMenezes/Chapter09.git
git push -u origin master
```

...or push an existing repository from the command line

```
git remote add origin https://github.com/AlissonMMenezes/Chapter09.git
git push -u origin master
```

Figure 9.6

Going back to the Visual Studio Code, I will add the remote URL to my local repository using the following command:

```
PS C:\Users\1511 MXTI\Chapter09> git remote add githubhttps://github.
com/AlissonMMenezes/Chapter09.git

PS C:\Users\1511 MXTI\Chapter09> git remote -v
github  https://github.com/AlissonMMenezes/Chapter09.git (fetch)
github  https://github.com/AlissonMMenezes/Chapter09.git (push)
```

Now that we have this configured, I can send the code to the remote repository. We call that action push, because the command that we will use is the git push:

```
PS C:\Users\1511 MXTI\Chapter09> git push github master
Enumerating objects: 9, done.
Counting objects: 100% (9/9), done.
Delta compression using up to 8 threads
Compressing objects: 100% (5/5), done.
Writing objects: 100% (9/9), 789 bytes | 394.00 KiB/s, done.
```

```
Total 9 (delta 1), reused 0 (delta 0), pack-reused 0

remote: Resolving deltas: 100% (1/1), done.

To https://github.com/AlissonMMenezes/Chapter09.git

* [new branch]      master -> master
```

The push command follows that sequence. `git push repo_name branch`. Now, we push the code to GitHub and the branch master. If we go back to GitHub, it is possible to see the code there:

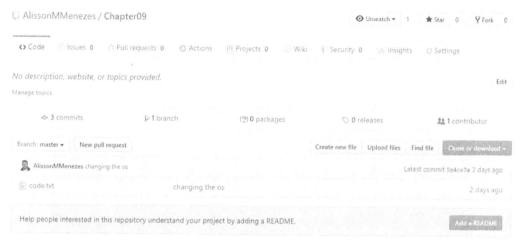

Figure 9.7

Now, it is so much easier to see what has changed, because we have a graphical interface with the number of commits, the branches and so much more information. Now, you can delete your local repository because your code is safe on GitHub.

I deleted my local repository and let's assume that I am a new developer. Now, I have to fetch the code from GitHub, make my changes, and push it back. However, when we are working in a team, it is a good practice to create a new branch, push my branch, and create a pull request. But, why that? We do that for another developer to do what we call code review. Thus, he will analyze your code and validate if it is in the good practices defined by the company.

As a new developer, the first thing I have to do is clone the repository using the following command:

```
PS C:\Users\1511 MXTI>git clone https://github.com/AlissonMMenezes/
Chapter09.git

Cloning into 'Chapter09'...

remote: Enumerating objects: 9, done.

remote: Counting objects: 100% (9/9), done.
```

```
remote: Compressing objects: 100% (4/4), done.
remote: Total 9 (delta 1), reused 9 (delta 1), pack-reused 0
Receiving objects: 100% (9/9), done.
Resolving deltas: 100% (1/1), done.
```

So, now we will create a new branch and edit the file:

```
PS C:\Users\1511 MXTI\Chapter09> git checkout -b new_feature
Switched to a new branch 'new_feature'
```

Following this, we have the new code:

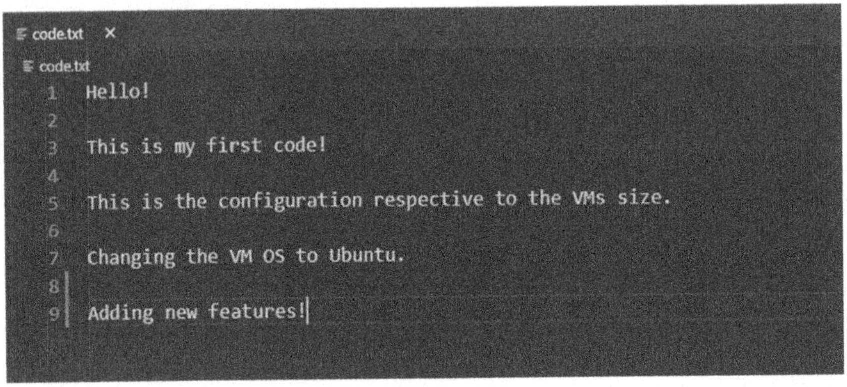

Figure 9.8

Now, we can commit and push to GitHub:

```
PS C:\Users\1511 MXTI\Chapter09> git add –all
PS C:\Users\1511 MXTI\Chapter09> git commit -m "adding new feature"
[new_feature 938b554] adding new feature
1 file changed, 3 insertions(+), 1 deletion(-)
PS C:\Users\1511 MXTI\Chapter09> git push origin new_feature
Enumerating objects: 5, done.
Counting objects: 100% (5/5), done.
Delta compression using up to 8 threads
Compressing objects: 100% (2/2), done.
Writing objects: 100% (3/3), 294 bytes | 294.00 KiB/s, done.
Total 3 (delta 1), reused 0 (delta 0), pack-reused 0
remote: Resolving deltas: 100% (1/1), completed with 1 local object.
remote:
```

```
remote: Create a pull request for 'new_feature' on GitHub by visiting:
remote:        https://github.com/AlissonMMenezes/Chapter09/pull/new/new_
feature
remote:
To https://github.com/AlissonMMenezes/Chapter09.git
* [new branch]        new_feature -> new_feature
```

The code was sent and the GitHub command returned as an URL:

https://github.com/AlissonMMenezes/Chapter09/pull/new/new_feature

That URL will redirect you to the new pull request page based on the branch that we just created. Let's take a look:

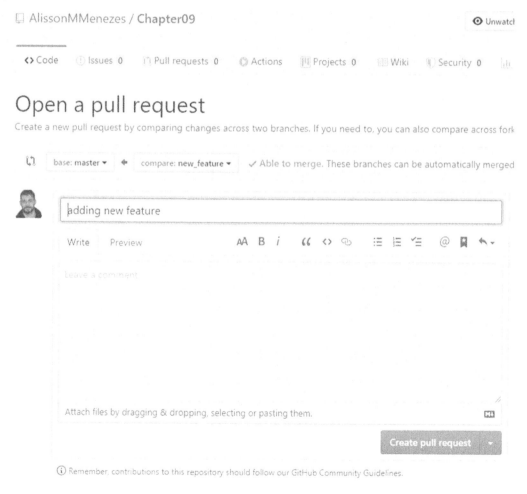

Figure 9.9

We can give a title that corresponds to what we've done. For example, it could be the name of your Jira task, something like DASF-158: changing the SSH keys. You can describe what you've done if you want, or just give a message for the code reviews. For example, please give a look at the lines between 55 and 99. I am not sure if my logic is correct. Now, you can create the `pull request`:

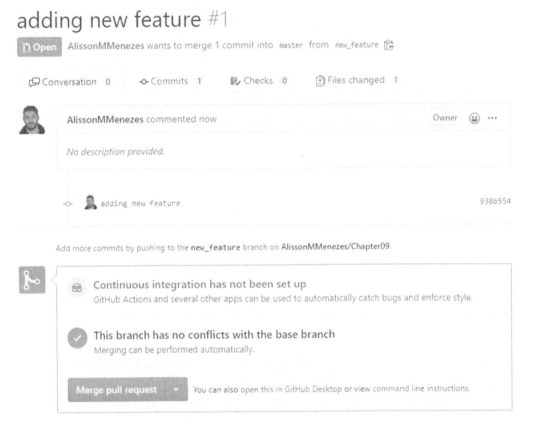

Figure 9.10

This is how a **PR (Pull Request)** looks like. And now, we can merge with the `master` branch or another branch we want to:

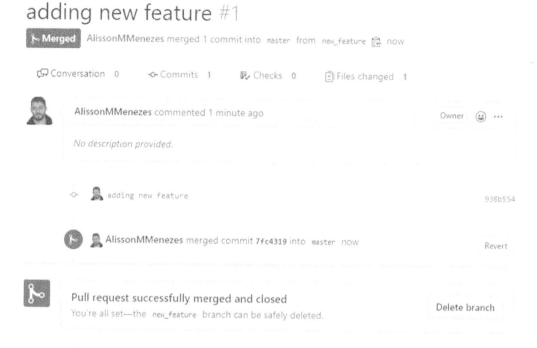

Figure 9.11

Conclusion

That was a really quick and short introduction to Git. But, I am pretty sure that it is enough for your daily tasks. Of course, in the real world, we will face many conflicts. As bigger the team is that you work with, more challenges and more complex will it be to manage the code, the branches, and the reviews. If you are in lucky work startup and you are the DevOps guy who is in charge of all the Cloud Infrastructure, this probably will attend to 100% of your necessities.

CHAPTER 10
Continuous Integration and Continuous Delivery Using Jenkins

This chapter aims to introduce you to the concept of Pipelines, **CI** (**Continuous Integration**), and **CD** (**Continuous Delivery**). It also gives an introduction to Jenkins, the most famous CI/CD platform and open-source.

Structure

In this chapter, we will discuss the following topics:

- Pipelines
- Continuous Integration
- Continuous Delivery
- Pipeline as Code and Jenkins

Objectives

After studying this unit, you should be able to:

- Know about DevOps pipelines
- Differentiate and how to implement CI/CD
- Create your pipelines as code using Groovy and Jenkins
- Deploy an application using Vagrant, Docker, and Jenkins

Pipelines

We can define a pipeline as a sequence of steps, which will take one thing from a starting point to an ending point, following a predefined path. In our case, when the code enters the pipeline, we have to check many things, like the code quality, best practices, running tests, generating a ZIP file, and it can be increased as much as you want. At the end of your pipeline, you will have your code with quality, following the best practices and ready to deploy everything in an automated way. It helps you improve the quality of your product or infrastructure, and speed up the process, as no one has to test each part of the pipeline. For some pipelines, the DevOps practices defined specific names, like Continuous Integration and Continuous Delivery.

Continuous Integration

Usually, when we are developing a software, we have many stages where our application goes through before reaching the end customer. Currently, we have these most common stages:

- **Development:** Where the developers can test the applications, fix bugs, and validate new feature requests. In this environment, we can break everything because it will not affect our end customers.

- **Staging:** A copy of the production environment, but just for the business team to validate the business rules if they follow the requirements defined by the clients. In this environment, we can have failures and new improvement requests. Following this is the last stage before it goes to the end customer.

- **Production:** This environment is where the application is in production, with everything validated, tested, and ready for our end customer. Of course, bugs can be found here, but the goal is to deliver the applications as much tested as we can to avoid problems.

The Continuous Integration pipeline is created to connect all the environment. For example, in the development stage, we have to follow some of the following tests:

- **Unit tests:** This test aims to validate the business rules for each part of our code, like classes, methods, functions, or whatsoever. But, these are the simplest tests that you can do in your application. For example, you can receive the task of creating a function where you need to sum 2 numbers. Your test will pass the numbers to that function and check if you are returning the expected result.

- **Integration tests:** Here, you will have to test a business case. For example, you created an API. Your end customer will make a request sending 2 parameters and he is expecting a JSON response with a product data. In this case, we do not need to check what is happening in the source code of your API, we just need to make sure that when we receive those 2 parameters, we will return the JSON with the product data.

- **End-to-end:** This is the hardest test that you have in your application. It will test your entire system, each functionality in detail impersonating a real customer. It takes a lot of time to be developed, so, most of the companies stop at the integration tests.

- **Quality test:** This test is used more to check the quality of your code. If you are following the best practices, if you are creating reusable codes, and not just copying and pasting code everywhere in your code, which will make the maintenance harder.

Of course, those tests that I explained are just common tests that you will find in most of the companies that you will work. However, there are more ways of testing applications. It can vary from project to project and company to company.

Once we pass in all these tests, we have to make our application go to other teams who will also test the application, many times in a manual way, to make sure that the developer understood what the requirements are and how we need to code our product. This is where we have the Continuous Delivery.

Continuous Delivery

In this stage, the developer did all work they were delegated to do. But, of course, we can have many communication problems between the client request and the software delivery.

Therefore, once all the tests were made by the developers, we can assume that we have a new version of our application, which can be called version 0.1. Assuming that it is working, we will create a package of that application and deploy it in the staging environment. In this environment, someone from the business part of the company will validate again if the feature requests are working properly as they requested. This stage is also used for the UX team to validate if your interface is understandable and easy to use. If this version of the application does not fulfill all the requirements, or the developers did not understand how the new feature should work, this version can be discarded and they will work in a new version called, 0.2. For example, and it will pass through all the environments again until it fulfills all the requirements specified by the end customer.

At the end of the day, Continuous Delivery is being able to deploy a version of your application every time a new feature is released. Not accumulating these features will be harder to test, since many are not uncommon for business areas validating the application manually.

Pipeline as Code and Jenkins

We have many tools which can help us with the pipelines and integration between the environment, and indeed Jenkins is the most famous, because of its flexibility that allows us to install many plugins to easily integrate with the Cloud providers and also being open source. Thus, we do not need to pay for a license.

The focus of this book is not especially software development, but Infrastructure as Code. So, all the examples that I will use will be regarding Infrastructure and how we can test and deploy it.

Firstly, we need to setup our Jenkins server. I will setup it using Vagrant. To create a VM with Ubuntu, install Docker, and then, Jenkins will run on top of the Docker:

```ruby
# -*- mode: ruby -*-
# vi: set ft=ruby :
Vagrant.configure("2") do |config|
  config.vm.box = "ubuntu/bionic64"
  config.vm.box_check_update = false
  config.vm.provider "virtualbox" do |vb|
    vb.memory = "1024"
  end

  config.vm.define "docker" do |docker|
    docker.vm.box = "ubuntu/bionic64"
    docker.vm.network "private_network", ip: "192.168.33.11"
    docker.vm.hostname = "docker"
    docker.vm.provision "shell", inline: <<-SHELL
      apt clean
      apt-get update
      apt-get remove docker docker-engine docker.io containerd runc -y
      apt-get install apt-transport-https ca-certificates curl gnupg-agent software-properties-common -y
      curl -fsSL https://download.docker.com/linux/ubuntu/gpg | apt-key add -
      add-apt-repository "deb [arch=amd64] https://download.docker.com/linux/ubuntu $(lsb_release -cs) stable"
      apt-get update -y
      apt-get install docker.io -y
    SHELL
  end
end
```

The preceding code is just edited a little bit from `chapter06`. Then, we already know how to install and run a VM on Vagrant. Now, I have a Docker environment running and to run the Jenkins in a container is very simple. Just run the following command:

```
root@docker:~# docker run -tdi --restart=always --name jenkins -p
8080:8080 -p 50000:50000 jenkins/jenkins:lts
```

After the containers start, you can access the Jenkins by the following address:

```
http://192.168.33.11:8080/login?from=%2F
```

It will show you the following screen asking for the initial password:

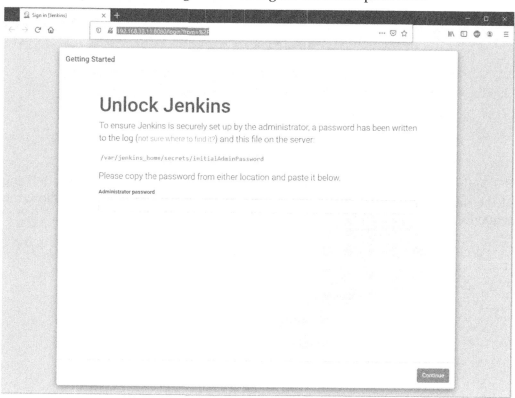

Figure 10.1

You can get the password by running the following command:

```
docker exec -ti jenkins cat /var/jenkins_home/secrets/
initialAdminPassword
```

a7a1b2c796404bceab99b014f3220a9a

You can just copy the password:

a7a1b2c796404bceab99b014f3220a9a

Paste in the screen and proceed with the installation.

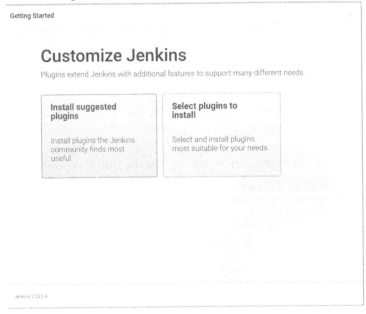

Figure 10.2

It is highly recommended to install the suggested plugins because it will install one of the most important, which is the git plugin. Now, you just need to follow the sequence, **Next**, **Next**, and **Finish**, to finalize your installation.

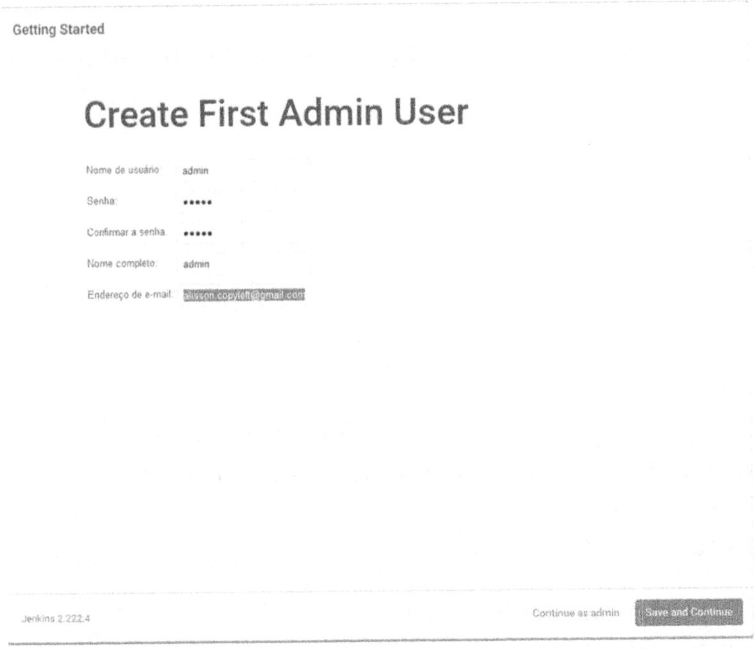

Getting Started

Create First Admin User

Nome de usuário:	admin
Senha:	•••••
Confirmar a senha:	•••••
Nome completo:	admin
Endereço de e-mail:	alisson.copyleft@gmail.com

Jenkins 2.222.4

Continue as admin   Save and Continue

Figure 10.3

The last part of the installation is setting your admin credentials. I have set `admin/`
`admin` for user and password. Finally, welcome to Jenkins:

Figure 10.4

Everyone who has worked with Jenkins knows that the UX is not one of Jenkins'
strengths. To work around this problem, there is a very famous plugin, called the
Blue Ocean to improve our interface and usability.

Go to **Manage Jenkins | Manage Plugins | Available** and **Search** for the Blue
Ocean:

Figure 10.5

Install the plugin and restart Jenkins. After everything, you will see a new button, Open Blue Ocean is available:

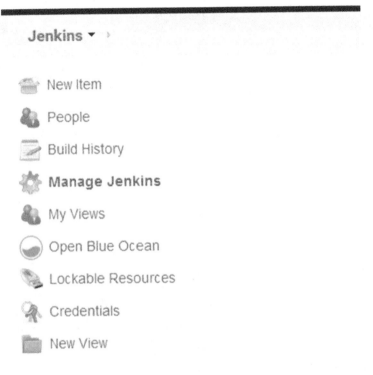

Figure 10.6

Click on the button and check the new interface:

Figure 10.7

From the initial screen, we can see that it is so much better. Of course, it is not mandatory to use this interface. It is just some sort of fancy feature, but I liked it. Not just for the interface, but it also makes mandatory the usage of a repository to versioning your pipelines. You can click on **Create a new Pipeline** and check it:

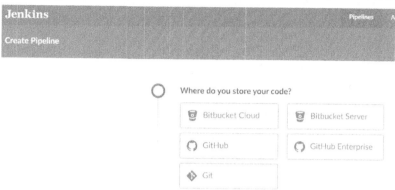

Figure 10.8

In my case, I will select **GitHub**, because I have already created a repository for this chapter. Creating the pipeline is pretty simple. You can just follow the steps showed in the screen followed, create an access token on GitHub, and bind it to your installation, like the preceding screenshot:

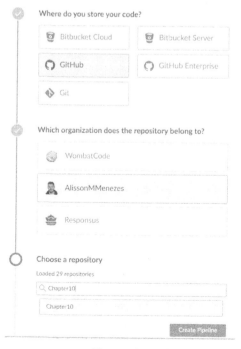

Figure 10.9

In the bound repository, you must have a file, called Jenkinsfile, in the root. The Jenkins will scan the files looking for that specific one, read the code, and run the pipeline. I already created one with the following code:

```
pipeline {
    agent   any;
    stages {
        stage('Code Quality') {
            steps {
                sh 'echo checking code quality'
            }
        }
        stage('Unit Tests') {
            steps {
                sh 'echo Testing the Applications'
            }
        }
        stage('Build') {
            steps {
            sh 'echo Creating application Package'
            }
        }
        stage('Delivery') {
            steps {
                sh 'echo Uploading the artifact to a repository'
            }
        }
        stage('Deploy') {
            steps {
                sh 'echo Deploying the Application'
            }
        }
    }
}
```

Jenkins uses the Groovy language to write the pipelines. It was a basic scaffold of what are the basics we need to have in our pipeline. Saving everything and checking the interface, you will see that the pipeline ran automatically and successfully:

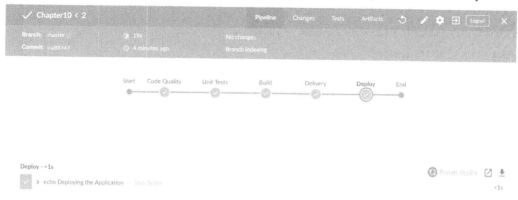

Figure 10.10

In the code, we just have some `echo` statements which are representing the real codes. Now, we need to replace them with a real application and real commands to check the application, test the application, and deploy it after all. However, of course, it will not be a complex application. Nevertheless, we will have everything, and here is what the application will do.

Create an API which will receive credit card transactions and to validate the transactions follow these criteria:

1. Validate if the credit card is active.

2. Validate if the transaction amount is above the credit card limit.

3. Validate if the transaction was approved.

The API must receive a JSON request in the following format:

```
{
  "status": true,
  "number":123456,
  "limit":1000,
  "transaction":{
    "amount":500
  }
}
```

Now, I developed everything using Flask, because is fast and easy. The API code is as follows:

```python
#!/usr/bin/python3

from flask import Flask, request, jsonify
from functools import wraps

app = Flask(__name__)

def check_card(f):
    wraps(f)
    def validation(*args, **kwargs):
        data = request.get_json()
        if not data.get("status"):
            response = {"approved":False,
            "newLimit":data.get("limit"),
            "reason":"Blocked Card"}
            return jsonify(response)

        if data.get("limit") < data.get("transaction").get("amount"):
            response = {"approved":False,
            "newLimit":data.get("limit"),
            "reason":"Transaction above the limit"}
            return jsonify(response)
        return f(*args, **kwargs)

    return(validation)

@app.route("/api/transaction",methods=["POST"])
@check_card
def transaction():
    card = request.get_json()
    new_limit = card.get("limit") - card.get("transaction").get("amount")
    response = {"approved":True,"newLimit":new_limit}
    return jsonify(response)

if __name__ == '__main__':
    app.run(debug=True)
```

The application is receiving the transactions and the validating via Python decorators. If tested manually, it works. But, it is very exhaustive to test everything every time. That is why, we create automated tests. In this case, I have 3 business rules that were already mentioned and here follows the code for those tests:

```python
#!/usr/bin/python3

import os
import tempfile

import pytest

from app import app

@pytest.fixture
def client():
    app.config['TESTING'] = True
    client = app.test_client()

    yield client

def test_valid_transaction(client):
    card = {
            "status": True,
            "number":123456,
            "limit":1000,
            "transaction":{
                "amount":500
            }
        }
    rv = client.post("/api/transaction",json=card)
    assert  True == rv.get_json().get("approved")
    assert  500 == rv.get_json().get("newLimit")


def test_above_limit(client):
    card = {
            "status": True,
            "number":123456,
            "limit":1000,
            "transaction":{
```

```
                    "amount":1500
            }
        }
    rv = client.post("/api/transaction",json=card)
    assert   False == rv.get_json().get("approved")
    assert   "Transaction above the limit" in rv.get_json().get("reason")


def test_blocked_card(client):
    card = {
            "status": False,
            "number":123456,
            "limit":1000,
            "transaction":{
                "amount":500
            }
        }
    rv = client.post("/api/transaction",json=card)
    assert   False == rv.get_json().get("approved")
    assert   "Blocked Card" in rv.get_json().get("reason")
```

Of course, I also need to install some external module which must be in the requirements.txt file:

```
pytest
flask
pylint
```

Now, you have the following three files:

```
app.py
test_app.py
requirements.txt
```

This belongs to the application and we have the Jekinsfile, which is not a part of the application, but it is important for the process, in general. The next step is to prepare the Jenkins environment to test the application. Of course, we do not need much, just the Python and the PIP to install the new modules. Then, you can run the following command within the container:

root@docker:~# docker exec -ti -u 0 jenkins apt clean

```
root@docker:~# docker exec -ti -u 0 jenkins apt update
root@docker:~# docker exec -ti -u 0 jenkins apt install python python-
pip -y
```

The parameter -u is new for us. It says to the Docker for which user we need to run the commands. In our case, the user represented by the UID 0, is the user root, the Jenkins default image. Therefore, the default user is the user Jenkins. We can validate it using the following commands:

```
root@docker:~# docker exec-ti jenkins whoami
jenkins
root@docker:~# docker exec-ti jenkins id
uid=1000(jenkins) gid=1000(jenkins) groups=1000(jenkins)
```

Going back to the pipeline topic, now, we need to replace the echo statements in the stages for the real commands which will be used. Then, the pipeline should be as follows:

```
pipeline {
    agent   any;
    stages {
        stage('Preparing the environment') {
            steps {
                sh 'python -m pip install -r requirements.txt'
            }
        }
        stage('Code Quality') {
            steps {
                sh 'python -m pylint app.py'
            }
        }
        stage('Tests') {
            steps {
                sh 'python -m pytest'
            }
        }
        stage('Build') {
            steps {
                sh 'exit 1'
```

```
            }
        }
        stage('Delivery') {
            steps {
                sh 'exit 1'
            }
        }
        stage('Deploy') {
            steps {
                sh 'exit 1'
            }
        }
    }
}
```

Make sure that everything is within your repository, like mine. You can check using the following link:

https://github.com/AlissonMMenezes/Chapter10

Run your pipeline manually. For now, we cannot trigger it automatically, because the Jenkins installation is local, and the GitHub is in the Cloud. However, we will see that in the next chapters.

In order to run the pipeline manually, you can open a new tab: `http://192.168.33.11:8080/`:

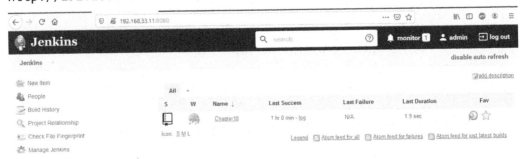

Figure 10.11

Click on the **Run** button, by side of the star. In your first attempt, it will raise the following error:

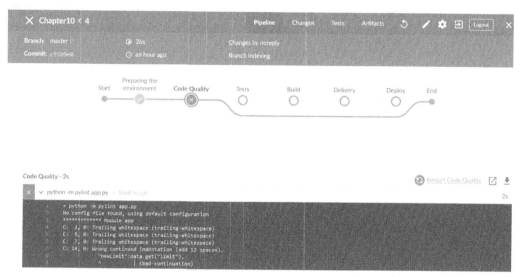

Figure 10.12

This error means the code is not following the code quality standards defined by the `pylint`. So, we need to fix it in order to go to the next stage of the pipeline. Fixing it is simple. There is a module, called `autopep8`, which can fix the code automatically for you. To install it, use the following command:

```
python -m pip install autopep8
```

PEP8 is a set of best practices for your Python code. You can check more details about it in by clicking on this link: **https://www.python.org/dev/peps/pep-0008/**

Fixing the code:

```
python -m autopep8 --in-place --aggressive --aggressive .\app.py
```

Most of the code was fixed, although, `autopep8` module fixes most of the indentation issues. If you run the `pylint` again, we can see that not everything was fixed. Therefore, the module cannot refactor your code. This is a developer's duty, but, we will do that here:

```
PS C:\Users\1511 MXTI\Pictures\Book\DevOps With Linux\Chapter10\VMs>
python -m pylint .\app.py
```

```
************ Module app
```

```
app.py:27:0: C0325: Unnecessary parens after 'return' keyword
(superfluous-parens)
```

```
app.py:1:0: C0114: Missing module docstring (missing-module-docstring)
```

```
app.py:9:0: C0103: Argument name "f" doesn't conform to snake_case
```

naming style (invalid-name)

app.py:9:0: C0116: Missing function or method docstring (missing-function-docstring)

app.py:32:0: C0116: Missing function or method docstring (missing-function-docstring)

app.py:4:0: C0411: standard import "from functools import wraps" should be placed before "from flask import Flask, request, jsonify" (wrong-import-order)

```
------------------------------------------------------------
```

Your code has been rated at 7.27/10 (previous run: 7.73/10, -0.45)

After fixing everything required by the `pylint` module, the code now is as follows:

```python
#!/usr/bin/python3
"""

This code is used as an example for the Chapter10 of the book DevOps
With Linux

"""

from functools import wraps
from flask import Flask, request, jsonify


APP = Flask(__name__)


def check_card(func):
    """

    This function validates the credit card transactions
    """

    wraps(func)

    def validation(*args, **kwargs):
        """

        This function is a decorator,
        which will return the function corresponding to the respective action
        """

        data = request.get_json()
        if not data.get("status"):
```

```
            response = {"approved": False,
                "newLimit": data.get("limit"),
                "reason": "Blocked Card"}
            return jsonify(response)

        if data.get("limit") < data.get("transaction").get("amount"):
            response = {"approved": False,
                "newLimit": data.get("limit"),
                "reason": "Transaction above the limit"}
            return jsonify(response)
        return func(*args, **kwargs)

    return validation

@APP.route("/api/transaction", methods=["POST"])
@check_card
def transaction():
    """

    This function is resposible to expose the endpoint for receiving the
    incoming transactions
    """

    card = request.get_json()
    new_limit = card.get("limit") - card.get("transaction").get("amount")
    response = {"approved": True, "newLimit": new_limit}
    return jsonify(response)

if __name__ == '__main__':
    APP.run(debug=True)
```

It is looking quite better, is it not? Remember that we refactored the code, and then, we need to change our tests as well. In the test source code, we just need to change the following part:

```
@pytest.fixture
def client():
    APP.config['TESTING'] = True
    client = APP.test_client()

    yield client
```

We are ready to run the pipeline again. Let's see how is the new behavior:

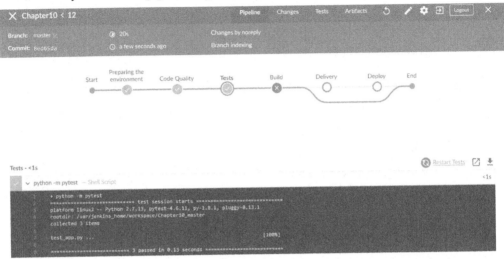

Figure 10.13

Now it is perfect! We passed the code quality check, the functional tests, and we are blocked at the build step. It makes sense, because I coded it to run an exit 1. For that step, we need to generate a new Docker image. With our application inside, deploy it in the same server that we are running our Jenkins container.

In order to do it, we can set up the VM as a Jenkins node. The address you must access to add a new node is as follows:

http://192.168.33.11:8080/computer/new

I will call that node as Docker server. The remote root directory must be /tmp, and the Labels Docker server as well. The Launch method must by the agent, connect to the master. Then, we will install the agent within the VM and it will be responsible to run the next steps of the pipeline:

Name	DockerServer
Description	
# of executors	1
Remote root directory	/tmp
Labels	DockerServer
Usage	Use this node as much as possible
Launch method	Launch agent by connecting it to the master

Figure 10.14

After configuring and saving the configuration, the Jenkins will make the agent available for you:

http://192.168.33.11:8080/computer/DockerServer/

 Agent DockerServer

Mark this node temporarily offline

Connect agent to Jenkins one of these ways:

- Launch Launch agent from browser
- Run from agent command line:

```
java -jar agent.jar -jnlpUrl http://192.168.33.11:8080/computer/DockerServer/slave-agent.jnlp -secret
c62147686c498dff6097c8fefa519c6ef249c7308e5b373c6258fd4eefbec7e5 -workDir "/tmp"
```

Run from agent command line, with the secret stored in a file:

```
echo c62147686c498dff6097c8fefa519c6ef249c7308e5b373c6258fd4eefbec7e5 > secret-file
java -jar agent.jar -jnlpUrl http://192.168.33.11:8080/computer/DockerServer/slave-agent.jnlp -secret
@secret-file -workDir "/tmp"
```

Projects tied to DockerServer

None

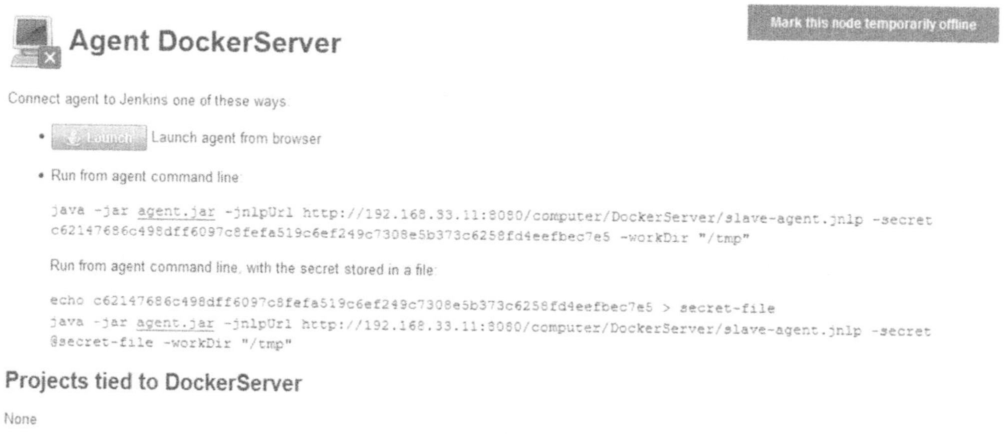

Figure 10.15

We can just copy and paste the line in the VM:

```
root@docker:~# apt install openjdk-8-jre-headless -y
root@docker:~# wget http://192.168.33.11:8080/jnlpJars/agent.jar

root@docker:~# java -jar agent.jar -jnlpUrl http://192.168.33.11:8080/
computer/DockerServer/slave-agent.jnlp -secret
1309b876151399817cab2ef0da0ea34716ecbc01a44b38a95c93fdd748d72629
-workDir "/tmp"
INFO: Agent discovery successful
Agent address: 192.168.33.11
Agent port:    50000
Identity:      52:84:5b:cb:ed:f7:98:4c:da:b2:64:66:48:de:cf:be
Jun 10, 2020 12:46:41 PM hudson.remoting.jnlp.Main$CuiListener status
INFO: Handshaking
Jun 10, 2020 12:46:41 PM hudson.remoting.jnlp.Main$CuiListener status
INFO: Connecting to 192.168.33.11:50000
Jun 10, 2020 12:46:41 PM hudson.remoting.jnlp.Main$CuiListener status
INFO: Trying protocol: JNLP4-connect
Jun 10, 2020 12:46:42 PM hudson.remoting.jnlp.Main$CuiListener status
INFO: Remote identity confirmed:
```

```
52:84:5b:cb:ed:f7:98:4c:da:b2:64:66:48:de:cf:be
Jun 10, 2020 12:46:43 PM hudson.remoting.jnlp.Main$CuiListener status
INFO: Connected
```

The agent is successfully connected. Now, we can continue to code the pipeline and finish the application deployment:

```
pipeline {
    agent   any;
    stages {
        stage('Preparing the environment') {
            steps {
                sh 'python -m pip install -r requirements.txt'
            }
        }
        stage('Code Quality') {
            steps {
                sh 'python -m pylint app.py'
            }
        }
        stage('Tests') {
            steps {
                sh 'python -m pytest'
            }
        }

        stage('Build') {
            agent {
                node{
                    label "DockerServer";
                }
            }
            steps {
                sh 'docker build https://github.com/AlissonMMenezes/
Chapter10.git -t chapter10:latest'
            }
        }
```

```
stage('Deploy') {
    agent {
        node{
            label "DockerServer";
        }
    }
    steps {
        sh 'docker run -tdi -p 5000:5000 chapter10:latest'
    }
}
```

}

This is the latest version of the pipeline. Let's run it and see if it will work:

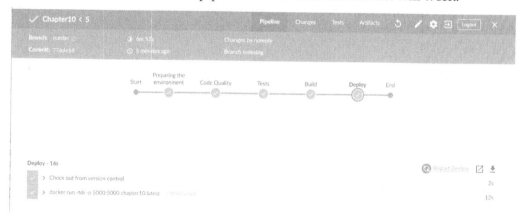

Figure 10.16

Great! Now we have a fully functional pipeline, versioned with an application, running tests, code quality, and also Dockerized.

Conclusion

We just learned how to create a pipeline as code using Jenkins, run code quality checks, functional tests, create an image based on a functional application, and deploy it on the top of a Docker server.

We could see that it is not an extremely hard task. Of course, as complex as is your project, more complex will be your pipeline. For example, in the initial steps, we were able to run everything on Jenkins by itself. By the final steps, we had to add a node and run on top of it. We also learned new information about Docker, for example, some parameters to start the container every time that the server has started. It is also possible to build an image using a Dockerfile hosted directly in a remote repository.

I am pretty sure this introduction will give you the start for creating your pipelines which will fit perfectly with your projects.

Questions

1.   What are the benefits of using pipelines?

2.   What are CI and CD?

3.   Why is it a good practice to use the pipeline as a code?

4.   What benefits can we have from the BlueOcean plugin?

5.   When are the Jenkins nodes needed?

Chapter 11

Deploying and Scaling Your Application Using Kubernetes

This chapter aims to introduce you to Kubernetes, showing how to create YAML files to deploy, and scale your applications with the most popular and reliable container orchestration tool.

Structure

In this chapter, we will discuss the following topics:

- Kubernetes
- Introduction to Kubernetes
- Deploying on Cloud

Objectives

After studying this unit, you should be able to:

- Know about Kubernetes
- Explain the benefits of Kubernetes
- Create YAML files to deploy your application
- Test your application running in the cluster

Kubernetes

Kubernetes is a container orchestration tool. In the previous chapters, we have been using Docker a lot for deploying applications, creating new images, etc. However, imagine if you have more than one hundred containers to manage. It is an impossible task for just one guy. The Docker, by itself, has the Docker Swarm, which helps you with that task. But, it is not commonly adopted by the market, since it misses some features and integrations that we have on Kubernetes. It was created by Google some years ago, based on a project, called Borg, which was also a container orchestration tool. With the release of Docker, that project was adapted to use it, and now it has become the official platform to manage your cluster.

Introduction to Kubernetes

Like the other chapters, our focus is always on how to implement it in the real-world. Let's have a short introduction of how we can setup our local environment to learn Kubernetes, and then, we can setup a real environment and deploy an application. You will see that the commands are same when we run it in our local environment and on the Cloud environment.

First of all, we will install minikube. It is a tool to set up a local Kubernetes environment on the top of a Virtual Box, like we have been doing along with the book:

wget https://github.com/kubernetes/minikube/releases/download/v1.11.0/ minikube-windows-amd64.exe -O minikube.exe

If you are using another OS, you can follow the official documentation: **https:// kubernetes.io/docs/tasks/tools/install-minikube/**

Then, we can start the cluster:

```
PS C:\Users\1511 MXTI>.\minikube.exe start
* minikube v1.11.0 on Microsoft Windows 10 Pro 10.0.19041 Build 19041
* Automatically selected the virtualbox driver
* Downloading VM boot image ...
* Starting control plane node minikube in cluster minikube
* Downloading Kubernetes v1.18.3 preload ...
* Creating virtualbox VM (CPUs=2, Memory=6000MB, Disk=20000MB) ...
* Preparing Kubernetes v1.18.3 on Docker 19.03.8 ...
* Verifying Kubernetes components...
* Enabled addons: default-storageclass, storage-provisioner
* Done! kubectl is now configured to use "minikube"
```

We also need to install the `kubectl`, a command which we will use to manage your cluster, for `dev`, `stg`, and `prd`. If you are using another operating system, you can follow the official documentation: **https://kubernetes.io/docs/tasks/tools/install-minikube/**

PS C:\Users\1511 MXTI> **wget** https://storage.googleapis.com/kubernetes-release/release/v1.18.3/bin/linux/amd64/kubectl -O kubectl.exe

To begin with, we can run a simple command to see how many clusters we have configured in our environment:

PS C:\Users\1511 MXTI>.\kubectl.exe config get-clusters

NAME

Minikube

For now, it is just the `minikube`. But we will have more, one important thing to know is where the `kubectl` get this informationfrom:

PS C:\Users\1511 MXTI>cat 'C:\Users\1511 MXTI\.kube\config'

After the `minikube` installs the `k8s` cluster, it configures within the `config` file, inside of `.kube` folder which is located in your home directory. All the authenticate information is located within that file. If you want to know everything running inside your cluster, you can run the following command:

PS C:\Users\1511 MXTI>.\kubectl.exe get pods --all-namespaces

NAMESPACE RESTARTS AGE	NAME	READY	STATUS	
kube-system 22m	coredns-66bff467f8-47cmx	1/1	Running	0
kube-system 22m	coredns-66bff467f8-6kmwl	1/1	Running	0
kube-system 22m	etcd-minikube	1/1	Running	0
kube-system 22m	kube-apiserver-minikube	1/1	Running	0
kube-system 22m	kube-controller-manager-minikube	1/1	Running	0
kube-system 22m	kube-proxy-hwn2p	1/1	Running	0
kube-system 22m	kube-scheduler-minikube	1/1	Running	0
kube-system 22m	storage-provisioner	1/1	Running	0

I used the parameter to get pods, and another parameter `-all-namespaces`. It shows us all the running containers in the cluster among all the namespaces. For now, we just have one, called `kube-system`. Before we move on with more commands, it is important to understand `pod`, namespace, and not just it.

- **POD:** It represents a set of one or more containers running.

- **NAMESPACE:** It is the logical separation among the objects. For example, in the same cluster I can have, `dev` - `stg` - `prd`, namespaces, each one running on different versions of the same application, or it could be, `project1`, `project2`, and `project3`. You can divide your cluster in as many namespaces as you want.

- **SERVICE:** This is a resource which you will use to connect the external world with your pods. If you remember the Docker chapter, we had to map the host port `8080` to the container port `8080`. But it was for only one container. On Kubernetes, we have a `POD` which can have one or more containers that can be destroyed and recreated at any time. However, we cannot lose the port mapping, that is, the `SERVICE` job, where we configure a `NODE` Port, which will redirect to a `POD` port, exactly in the same way we did with Docker. It was one of the usages of the services, but, we can also have other implementations, like a load balancer, which has a `clusterIP` that will receive the incoming connections and forward it to the containers.

- **DEPLOYMENT:** It is a set of rules to make sure that you have a specific number of running containers. All the containers are running the same image, and if any container dies, it will be recreated. In other words, it will create your `PODs` automatically, and the `REPLICASET` will ensure the running containers.

- **INGRESS:** This resource can be compared to a Virtual Host, like we did in the Apache chapter. Here, we will have a `NAME`, which will point to `SERVICE`, which will point to a `POD`. If you are not using a DNS, the `INGRESS` is not mandatory.

The aforementioned items are called the Kubernetes objects. There are so many more objects that we can explore to understand more about Kubernetes, but we could write a whole book just explaining it. For now, I think it is enough to deploy some micro-services at last. If you are deploying stateful applications, you will probably have to extend your reading to `VOLUMES`.

So, now we can create the first `NAMESPACE` and start to play around some objects:

```
PS C:\Users\1511 MXTI>.\kubectl.exe create namespace chapter11
namespace/chapter11 created
PS C:\Users\1511 MXTI> .\kubectl.exe get ns
NAME                STATUS    AGE
```

```
chapter11         Active    11s
default           Active    38m
kube-node-lease   Active    38m
kube-public       Active    38m
kube-system       Active    38m
```

Notice that we can use the full form of the parameters, and also the short form, like, when I listed the namespaces, I used just the ns.

The INGRESS is a separate resource from Kubernetes. When you are using it on the Cloud, some give it to you already installed. But, in an on-premises environment, you usually have to install. For our local environment, we will have to install it using the following command:

```
PS C:\Users\1511 MXTI>.\minikube.exe addons enable ingress
* The 'ingress' addon is enabled
```

To run your first application in the cluster, run the following command:

```
PS C:\Users\1511 MXTI>.\minikube.exe addons enable ingress

PS C:\Users\1511 MXTI>.\kubectl.exe --namespace=chapter11 run python
-dti --port=8080 --image=alissonmenezes/python:latest -l app=python
```

This command will download the python_app:v1 from my personal repository alissonmenezes and expose the port 8080. If you want to check if the pod is running, you can use the following command:

```
PS C:\Users\1511 MXTI>kubectl get pods --namespace=chapter11
NAME      READY   STATUS    RESTARTS   AGE
python    1/1     Running   1          6m43s
```

Now we have one pod running with one container in it. However, we want to access the application, but at this moment it is available only inside the cluster. The other applications inside the cluster are already capable of accessing it, but for us, from the outside, we will have to create a service for it:

```
PS C:\Users\1511 MXTI>.\kubectl.exe --namespace=chapter11 create service
clusterip python --tcp=80:8080
service/python created
```

We just created the SERVICE with clusterip type. It does not expose the NODE port, and we need the ingress to make the mapping from the outside to the inside of the cluster. Create a file called app.yaml with the following content:

```
apiVersion: extensions/v1beta1
```

```
kind: Ingress
metadata:
    name: python
    namespace: chapter11
    annotations:
        nginx.ingress.kubernetes.io/rewrite-target: /
spec:
    backend:
        serviceName: python
        servicePort: 80
```

The INGRESS is composed of Nginx server, which we call the "Ingress Controller". It is basically doing a proxy pass of the incoming connections from any addresses or names being forwarded to a service, called Python.

To apply the file, you must use the following command:

PS C:\Users\1511 MXTI>.\kubectl.exe apply -f .\app.yaml

ingress.extensions/python created

To get the minikube IP address, run the following command:

PS C:\Users\1511 MXTI>.\minikube ip

192.168.99.101

If you type this address on your web browser, you must see the following page:

Figure 11.1

The application is running!

We have successfully created everything using the commands and just the Ingress using a YAML file. However, it is possible to create everything just using the files that are the most used way to deploy everything on Kubernetes, because we can version the files and run it on the pipeline as we did in the previous chapter.

We can create everything in one file as follows:

```
---
apiVersion: apps/v1
kind: Deployment
metadata:
    name: python
    namespace: chapter11
    labels:
        app: python
spec:
    replicas: 1
    selector:
        matchLabels:
            app: python
    template:
        metadata:
            labels:
                app: python
spec:
    containers:
        - name: python
          image: alissonmenezes/python:latest
        ports:
            - containerPort: 8080
---
apiVersion: v1
kind: Service
metadata:
    labels:
        app: python
        name: python
        namespace: chapter11
spec:
    ports:
```

```
  - name: http
      port: 80
      protocol: TCP
      targetPort: 8080
  selector:
      app: python
      type: ClusterIP
---
apiVersion: extensions/v1beta1
kind: Ingress
metadata:
    name: python
    labels:
        app: python
        namespace: chapter11
    annotations:
        nginx.ingress.kubernetes.io/rewrite-target: /
spec:
    backend:
        serviceName: python
        servicePort: 80
```

To make sure that everything will run properly, you can delete everything:

```
PS C:\Users\1511 MXTI>.\kubectl.exe delete all -l app=python --all-namespaces
pod "python-779879dbb6-w57pr" deleted
```

Apply the file with the whole content:

```
PS C:\Users\1511 MXTI>.\kubectl.exe apply -f .\app.yaml
deployment.apps/python created
service/python created
ingress.extensions/python unchanged
```

Now, you already know the basics. Let's see it deploying in a real environment.

Deploying on Cloud

In order to deploy on the Cloud, we will use exactly the same app.yaml that we have been using until now. But firstly, we need to create the Kubernetes cluster. I will use the GCP for it.

I have created a project, called `chapter11`, where I will provision the cluster:

```
PS C:\Users\1511 MXTI>gcloud config set project chapter11-280417
Updated property [core/project].
```

Define where the compute nodes will be created:

```
PS C:\Users\1511 MXTI>gcloud config set compute/zone us-central1-c
Updated property [compute/zone].
```

Define where the compute nodes will be created:

```
PS C:\Users\1511 MXTI>gcloud container clusters create chapter11 --num-nodes=1
```

NAME	LOCATION	MASTER_VERSION	MASTER_IP	MACHINE_TYPE
NODE_VERSION	NUM_NODES	STATUS		
chapter11	us-central1-c	1.14.10-gke.36	35.193.191.37	n1-standard-1
1.14.10-gke.36	1	RUNNING		

Once the cluster is running, we need to login into the cluster using the following command:

```
PS C:\Users\1511 MXTI>gcloud container clusters get-credentials chapter11
Fetching cluster endpoint and auth data.
kubeconfig entry generated for chapter11.
```

And just like that, everything is perfect. Now, we can work exactly as we worked with `minikube`:

```
PS C:\Users\1511 MXTI>.\kubectl.exe config get-clusters
NAME

minikube

gke_chapter11-280417_us-central1-c_chapter11
```

By running the same command, we can see that we have another cluster configured, called `gke_chapter11`. When we ran the command `get-credentials`, the gke was set by default, and now, we do not need to think about running the commands in one cluster or another.

We also can check what is running with the following command:

```
PS C:\Users\1511 MXTI>.\kubectl.exe get pods --all-namespaces
NAMESPACE       NAME
READY    STATUS    RESTARTS    AGE
kube-system     event-exporter-v0.2.5-599d65f456-v2h9f
```

```
2/2      Running   0              4m50s
kube-system    fluentd-gcp-scaler-bfd6cf8dd-c4b6c
1/1      Running   0              4m42s
kube-system    fluentd-gcp-v3.1.1-pj6pp
2/2      Running   0              3m51s
kube-system    heapster-gke-7bff5f7474-9vgtb
3/3      Running   0              3m42s
kube-system    kube-dns-5995c95f64-742kn
4/4      Running   0              4m53s
kube-system    kube-dns-autoscaler-8687c64fc-w7w2d
1/1      Running   0              4m41s
kube-system    kube-proxy-gke-chapter11-default-pool-e3952147-h0gc
1/1      Running   0              4m41s
kube-system    l7-default-backend-8f479dd9-tpmk6
1/1      Running   0              4m53s
kube-system    metrics-server-v0.3.1-5c6fbf777-4xmlf
2/2      Running   0              4m5s
kube-system    prometheus-to-sd-692dh
2/2      Running   0              4m41s
kube-system    stackdriver-metadata-agent-cluster-level-79974b544-8n5gg
2/2      Running   0              3m58s
```

There are so many more pods running. If we compare with `minikube`, one example is the `stackdriver`, which is the Google tool to retrieve the logs from your cluster. Let's create the namespace:

```
PS C:\Users\1511 MXTI>.\kubectl.exe create namespace chapter11

namespace/chapter11 created
```

In the case of Google Kubernetes Engine, they have a Load Balancer as a service and it can be attached to our Kuberntes `SERVICE`. Thus, the service will have an external address, and we can point the DNS directly to it. In this case, we do not need the Ingress. Therefore, let's change this:

```
apiVersion: apps/v1
kind: Deployment
metadata:
    name: python
    namespace: chapter11
    labels:
        app: python
spec:
    replicas: 1
```

```
selector:
    matchLabels:
        app: python
template:
    metadata:
        labels:
            app: python
spec:
    containers:
    - name: python
        image: alissonmenezes/python:latest
    ports:
        - containerPort: 8080
```

As you can see the last line from the service part. Deploy the application:

```
PS C:\Users\1511 MXTI>.\kubectl.exe apply -f .\app.yaml
deployment.apps/python created
service/python created
```

Check if the pods are running with the following command:

```
PS C:\Users\1511 MXTI>.\kubectl.exe get pods -n chapter11
NAME                         READY   STATUS    RESTARTS   AGE
python-5bb87bbb45-6hwv7      1/1     Running   0          23s
```

Then, check if the service already has an external IP:

```
PS C:\Users\1511 MXTI>.\kubectl.exe get svc -n chapter11
NAME     TYPE           CLUSTER-IP      EXTERNAL-IP    PORT(S)        AGE
python   LoadBalancer   10.47.252.232   34.71.206.1    80:31693/TCP   68s
```

You must see the following page:

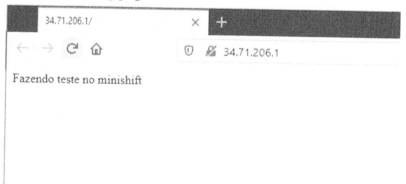

Figure 11.2

In the end, if you do not want to spend more money running this, you can delete the cluster by running the following command:

```
PS C:\Users\1511 MXTI>gcloud container clusters delete chapter11

The following clusters will be deleted.

- [chapter11] in [us-central1-c]


Do you want to continue (Y/n)?  y


Deleting cluster chapter11...|
```

Conclusion

This chapter introduced to you the basic steps of Kubernetes. It was a very short introduction. As I mentioned earlier, it is possible to write an entire book about Kubernetes. The goal here is just to deploy an application as an example and see how it works in your local environment and on the cloud using GKE.

I recommend you to read more about Kubernetes and Istio. You will discover amazing things, like fine-grain routes, A/B tests, canary deployment, going deep into the deployment strategies, and so much more.

I have a post in my personal blog giving a short introduction to Istio. You can translate the page using Google Chrome and see what we are doing.

https://alissonmachado.com.br/istio-e-minikube-teste-a-b/

Questions

1. What is the tool used to orchestrate a large number of containers?
2. What is the name of the Kubernetes object to map a node port to a container port?
3. What is the Kubernetes object that represents one or more containers?
4. What is the Kubernetes command to apply a YAML file?
5. What does Ingress do?

CHAPTER 12
Logs with Open-Source Tools

This chapter aims to introduce you to the EFK stack, showing how you can retrieve the application logs, send them to a centralized server, and visualize in a dashboard.

Structure

In this chapter, we will discuss the following topics:

- EFK stack
- Setup the EFK stack
- Shipping and centralizing logs with Fluentd and Elasticsearch
- Visualizing logs with Kibana

Objectives

After studying this unit, you should be able to:

- Know about EFK stack
- Send logs to an elasticsearch using Fluentd
- Search for the logs using Kibana
- Create alerts

EFK

Elasticsearch, Fluentd, and Kibana; this stack is famous around the Kubernetes environments. Often, we can see a DaemonSet of FluentD running on all the nodes retrieving the logs and sending them to an Elasticsearch Server which will index the logs and parse them, thus, making it easy to search the specific events based on your criteria. Kibana is the web interface that can be connected to an elasticsearch in order to visualize the data. Otherwise, we would have to make requests to the elasticsearch API. Kibana also gives us many features, like creating graphics based on logs. Thus, we can create visualizations of how many errors the application raised in the last two hours. Or, in another example, we could count the HTTP status codes and order them based on the number of requests. 40 requests returned status 400, 500 requests return status 200, 10 requests returned status 500, etc.

Setup the EFK Stack

We will have the following scenario; we are going to set up the elastichsearch and Kibana in a virtual machine using Vagrant and the Fluentd will run within our minikube cluster to ship the logs from the running applications to the remote server, and we will visualize it in a centralized way.

The Vagrant file is as follows:

```ruby
# -*- mode: ruby -*-
# vi: set ft=ruby :


# All Vagrant configuration is done below. The "2" in Vagrant.configure
# configures the configuration version (we support older styles for
# backwards compatibility). Please don't change it unless you know what
# you're doing.
Vagrant.configure("2") do |config|

  config.vm.box = "ubuntu/bionic64"

  config.vm.define "efk" do |efk|

    efk.vm.network "private_network", ip: "192.168.99.50"

    efk.vm.hostname = "efk"

    config.vm.provider "virtualbox" do |v|

      v.memory = 4096

    end
```

```
    efk.vm.provision "shell", inline: <<-SHELL

      apt clean

        wget -qO - https://artifacts.elastic.co/GPG-KEY-Elasticsearch |
apt-key add -

      apt-get install apt-transport-https -y

      echo "deb https://artifacts.elastic.co/packages/7.x/apt stable main"
| tee -a /etc/apt/sources.list.d/elastic-7.x.list

      apt-get update

      apt-get install Elasticsearch kibana -y

     #sed -i "s/#network.host: 192.168.0.1/network.host: 0.0.0.0/g" /etc/
Elasticsearch/Elasticsearch.yml

     #sed -i "s/#discovery.seed_hosts: \[\"host1\", \"host2\"\]/discovery.
seed_hosts: \[\]/g" /etc/Elasticsearch/Elasticsearch.yml

      #sed -i "s/#server.host: \"localhost\"/server.host: \"0.0.0.0\"/g"
/etc/kibana/kibana.yml

      #/etc/init.d/kibana restart

      #/etc/init.d/Elasticsearch start

    SHELL

  end

end
```

Provision your VM using the following command:

```
vagrant up --provision
```

When the server is ready, we have to change some configurations. First, enable the elasticsearch to listen to all the addresses by the following command:

```
sed -i "s/#network.host: 192.168.0.1/network.host: 0.0.0.0/g" /etc/
Elasticsearch/Elasticsearch.yml
```

Second, change the seed hosts by the following command:

```
sed -i "s/#discovery.seed_hosts: \[\"host1\", \"host2\"\]/discovery.
seed_hosts: \[\]/g" /etc/Elasticsearch/Elasticsearch.yml
```

Third, you must define that it is a single node cluster by the following command:

```
echo "discovery.type: single-node">> /etc/Elasticsearch/Elasticsearch.
yml
```

Fourth, change the Kibana configuration to listen to all the addresses as well by the following command:

```
sed -i "s/#server.host: \"localhost\"/server.host: \"0.0.0.0\"/g" /etc/
kibana/kibana.yml
```

Then, you can restart the services by running the following command:

```
root@efk:~# /etc/init.d/kibanarestart
d/Elasticsearch start
kibana started
root@efk:~# /etc/init.d/Elasticsearchstart
[....] Starting Elasticsearch (via systemctl): Elasticsearch.service
```

If you did all the steps correctly, you can check the service ports using the command ss -ntpl:

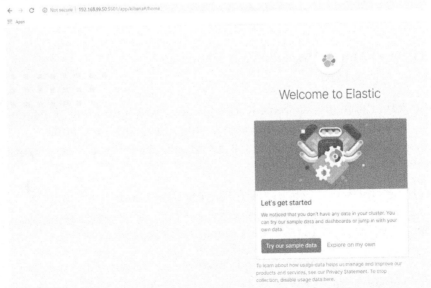

Figure 12.1

The Kibana is running on port 5601. Now, you can use the following address to check the interface.

```
http://192.168.99.50:5601
```

Figure 12.2

The server takes a while to start. If it takes about 10 minutes, do not worry.

At this moment, we do not have to do anything else in this server, so, let's go to the minikube and run the FluentD to ship the logs. After that, we will come back to the Kibana server and see the logs.

Running Fluentd

First of all, let's setup the `minikube` environment with the following command:

```
PS C:\Users\1511 MXTI\Documents\Blog\EKF> minikube delete
* Deleting "minikube" in virtualbox ...
* Removed all traces of the "minikube" cluster.


PS C:\Users\1511 MXTI\Documents\Blog\EKF> minikube.exestart
* minikube v1.11.0 on Microsoft Windows 10 Pro 10.0.19041 Build 19041
* Automatically selected the virtualbox driver
* Starting control plane node minikube in cluster minikube
* Creating virtualbox VM (CPUs=2, Memory=6000MB, Disk=20000MB) ...
* Preparing Kubernetes v1.18.3 on Docker 19.03.8 ...
* Verifying Kubernetes components...
* Enabled addons: default-storageclass, storage-provisioner
* Done! kubectl is now configured to use "minikube"
```

I deleted my existing environment and started a fresh environment to make sure that we have exactly the same environment. With the Kubernetes environment running, we will set up the `DaemonSet` using the following file:

```
apiVersion: apps/v1
kind: DaemonSet
metadata:
    name: fluentd
    namespace: kube-system
    labels:
        k8s-app: fluentd-logging
        version: v1
spec:
    selector:
        matchLabels:
            name: fluentd
    template:
```

```yaml
      metadata:
        labels:
          name: fluentd
          k8s-app: fluentd-logging
          version: v1
          kubernetes.io/cluster-service: "true"
spec:
  containers:
    - name: fluentd
      image: fluent/fluentd-kubernetes-daemonset:v1-debian-
Elasticsearch
      env:
        - name: FLUENT_ELASTICSEARCH_HOST
          value: "192.168.99.50"
        - name: FLUENT_ELASTICSEARCH_SSL_VERIFY
          value: "false"
        - name: FLUENT_ELASTICSEARCH_PORT
          value: "9200"
        - name: FLUENT_ELASTICSEARCH_SCHEME
          value: "http"
        - name: FLUENT_UID
          value: "0"
        - name: FLUENT_LOGSTASH_FORMAT
          value: "true"
        - name: FLUENT_LOGSTASH_PREFIX
          value: "fluentd"
        - name: FLUENTD_SYSTEMD_CONF
          value: "disable"
      resources:
        limits:
          memory: 200Mi
          requests:
            cpu: 100m
            memory: 200Mi
      volumeMounts:
        - name: varlog
        mountPath: /var/log
        - name: varlibdockercontainers
        mountPath: /var/lib/docker/containers
        readOnly: true
        terminationGracePeriodSeconds: 30
```

```
volumes:
  - name: varlog
    hostPath:
      path: /var/log
  - name: varlibdockercontainers
    hostPath:
        path: /var/lib/docker/containers
```

DaemonSet: It is a Kubernetes object which is responsible to run the same pod on every node of the cluster. The difference between a normal pod and a DaemonSet is that a pod is mandatory on every node, if you are deploying an application, not necessary you have to run the application on all nodes:

```
kubectl apply -f .\fluentd.yaml
```

```
daemonset.apps/fluentd configured
```

The preceding command will run the DaemonSet in your cluster. To check if it is running, you can run the following command:

```
PS C:\Users\1511 MXTI\DataLake> kubectl get daemonset -n kube-system
```

NAME	DESIRED	CURRENT	READY	UP-TO-DATE	AVAILABLE	NODE SELECTOR	AGE
fluentd	1	1	1	1	1	<none>	7m26s
kube-proxy	1	1	1	1	1	kubernetes.io/os=linux	13h

It is important to check the logs, because starting from now, the logs must be sent to the elasticsearch server:

```
PS C:\Users\1511 MXTI\DataLake> kubectl logs  daemonset/fluentd -n kube-system
```

Visualizing the Logs

Now, we can go back to the Kibana dashboard, because the logs must have already been shipped to the server. The next goal is to visualize them. In the initial page, click on the option *Explore on my own*. Then, click on the top left and discover the logs:

Figure 12.3

Now, we can create an index that matches with all the logs stored. We can do that once that cluster is used only for this Kubernetes environment. If you will use the same elasticsearch for all the logs of the company, it would be better to create different indexes for each case:

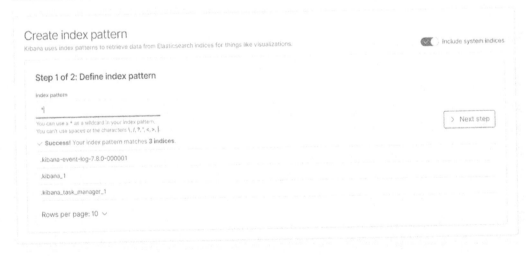

Figure 12.4

We must define the **Index Pattern as ***, which will get all the logs:

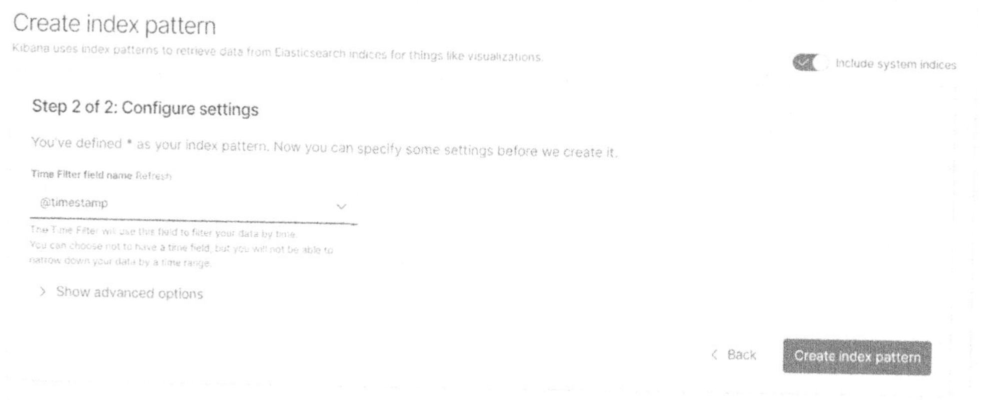

Figure 12.5

You can select the time filter as a timestamp. If we go again to the discovery part and select logs from 3 months ago, we will be able to see that the logs are already in the Elasticsearch. Of course, we do not need to put 3 months ago, but I just wanted to make sure that we will see all the present logs:

Figure 12.6

If you look on the left side, you can find some Kubernetes elements. You can play around that because, now, we do not need to access the Kubernetes cluster to access the logs.

Let's deploy an application and see how we can check the logs:

```
Kubectl create ns chapter11
```

Create a namespace, called *Chapter11: Deploying and Scaling your Application using Kubernetes*, because we will use the same application used in the last chapter. The yaml file for the application is as follows:

```
apiVersion: apps/v1
kind: Deployment
metadata:
    name: python
    namespace: chapter11
    labels:
        app: python
spec:
    replicas: 1
    selector:
        matchLabels:
            app: python
    template:
    metadata:
        labels:
            app: python
spec:
    containers:
    - name: python
        image: alissonmenezes/python:latest
    ports:
        - containerPort: 8080
---
apiVersion: v1
kind: Service
metadata:
    labels:
        app: python
        name: python
    namespace: chapter11
spec:
    ports:
    - name: http
        port: 80
        protocol: TCP
        targetPort: 8080
    selector:
        app: python
```

```
    type: ClusterIP
---
apiVersion: extensions/v1beta1
kind: Ingress
metadata:
    name: python
    labels:
        app: python
        namespace: chapter11
    annotations:
        nginx.ingress.kubernetes.io/rewrite-target: /
spec:
    backend:
        serviceName: python
        servicePort: 80
```
Run the following command now:

```
PS C:\Users\1511 MXTI\Documents\Blog\EKF> minikube.exe ip
192.168.99.102
```

The Kubernetes IP is `192.168.99.102`. We will use it to access the application. Make sure that you have enabled the ingress with the following command:

```
PS C:\Users\1511 MXTI\DataLake> minikube.exe addons enable ingress
* The 'ingress' addon is enabled
```

If we access the application on the browser, we will see the following page:

Figure 12.7

If we go to the applications logs on Kubernetes, we can see the following:

```
PS C:\Users\1511 MXTI\DataLake> kubectl logs deploy/python -n chapter11
* Running on http://0.0.0.0:8080/ (Press CTRL+C to quit)
* Restarting with stat
* Debugger is active!
* Debugger PIN: 954-738-244
172.17.0.6 - - [28/Jun/2020 10:22:16] "GET / HTTP/1.1" 200 -
172.17.0.6 - - [28/Jun/2020 10:22:17] "GET /favicon.ico HTTP/1.1" 404 -
172.17.0.6 - - [28/Jun/2020 10:22:18] "GET / HTTP/1.1" 200 -
172.17.0.6 - - [28/Jun/2020 10:22:18] "GET / HTTP/1.1" 200 -
```

It means that we generated some logs, and then we can see those on the Kibana. Let's give a look. First, we need the pod name:

```
PS C:\Users\1511 MXTI\DataLake> kubectl get pods -n chapter11
NAME                      READY   STATUS    RESTARTS   AGE
python-779879dbb6-wrw2g   1/1     Running   0          44m
```

And the query on Kibana will be like this:

```
kubernetes.pod_name:python-779879dbb6-wrw2g
```

The syntax is: `key : value.` Then, the first parameter is the respective element that you want to filter. The colon, `:` , represents the equal and in the end, you have the value used as a criteria.

The Kibana page you will see will be like the following screenshot:

Figure 12.8

Let's analyze the log because we have an important information to check:

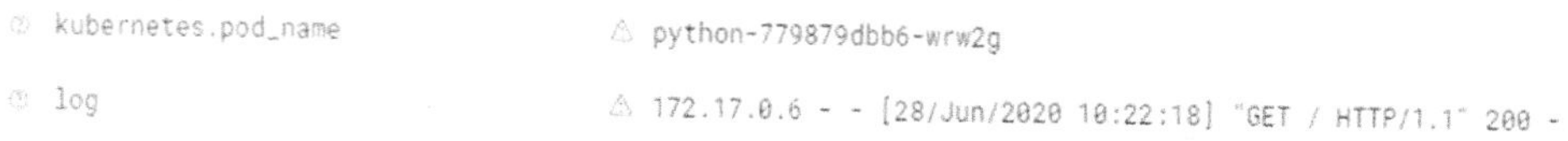
kubernetes.pod_name
python-779879dbb6-wrw2g
log
172.17.0.6 - - [28/Jun/2020 10:22:18] "GET / HTTP/1.1" 200 -

Figure 12.9

Pay attention, the `pod_name` matches with the criteria, and the log has the logline that we saw on the Kubernetes. Now, we are sure that the logs were sent to elasticsearch. We can visualize them on Kibana and now, we can create a specific visualization to simplify the log analysis.

Creating alerts

With the logs within the elasticsearch and we know how to find them, let's create some alerts which will notify us when an event happens. The event can be defined by you, can return a status `404`, status `500`, or for example, part of an error message.

In our case, every time that someone tries to access a non-existing page, it will return the `404` status and it will send a notification. In order to do that, we will use a tool called **ElastAlert**. It is a tool in Python which will connect to our elasticsearch, will read the logs, and send the notifications.

Within the EFK stack, let's install it.

```
root@efk:~# apt install python3-pip -y
root@efk:~# python3 -m pip install elastalert
```

Sometimes, we may face an issue because of the other modules version. The most important module for the `ElastAlert` is the PyYAML. So, let's upgrade it to make sure that we are using the latest version:

```
root@efk:~# python3 -m pip install PyYAML --upgrade
```

Once ElastAlert is installed, we need to connect it with elasticsearch. To do it, run the following command:

```
root@efk:~# elastalert-create-index
Enter Elasticsearch host: 127.0.0.1
Enter Elasticsearch port: 9200
Use SSL? t/f: f
Enter optional basic-auth username (or leave blank):
Enter optional basic-auth password (or leave blank):
Enter optional Elasticsearch URL prefix (prepends a string to the URL of
every request):
```

```
New index name? (Default elastalert_status)
New alias name? (Default elastalert_alerts)
Name of existing index to copy? (Default None)
Elastic Version: 7.8.0
Reading Elastic 6 index mappings:
Reading index mapping 'es_mappings/6/silence.json'
Reading index mapping 'es_mappings/6/elastalert_status.json'
Reading index mapping 'es_mappings/6/elastalert.json'
Reading index mapping 'es_mappings/6/past_elastalert.json'
Reading index mapping 'es_mappings/6/elastalert_error.json'
New index elastalert_status created
Done!
```

So, the next step is to create the config.yaml, which is the file where the elasticsearch server is configured:

```
root@efk:~# cat config.yaml
rules_folder: rules


run_every:
minutes: 1

buffer_time:
minutes: 15

es_host: 127.0.0.1
es_port: 9200
writeback_index: elastalert_status
writeback_alias: elastalert_alerts

alert_time_limit:
days: 2
```

Now, we need to create a rule. The ElastAlert will run the query every minute checking if we have the logs which match the criteria. Create a folder, called rules with the following command:

```
root@efk:~# ls
config.yaml   rules
```

```
root@efk:~# mkdir rules
root@efk:~# pwd
/root
```

Within the rules folder, create a file, called `alert_404.yml` with the following content:

```
es_host: 192.168.99.50
es_port: 9200
name: Alerting 404
type: frequency
index: "*"
num_events: 1
timeframe:
hours: 24
filter:
- query:
    wildcard:
        log: "404"
alert:
    - slack:
        slack_webhook_url: "https://hooks.slack.com/services/
T016B1J0J2J/B0830S98KSL/TAlTSxL2IhpCRyIVFOxdtVbZ"
```

I created a workspace on Slack, where I created a web hook. If you want to know more about that, you can check the documentation later on. But, for now, the most important thing is to see if it is working. So, let's run the `ElastAlert` with the following command:

```
root@efk:~# elastalert --rule rules/alert_404.yml --verbose
1 rules loaded
INFO:elastalert:Starting up
INFO:elastalert:Disabled rules are: []
INFO:elastalert:Sleeping for 9.999665 seconds
```

Now, you can try to access a non-existing page, like the following screenshot:

Not Found

The requested URL was not found on the server. If you entered the URL manually please check your spelling and try again.

Figure 12.10

This access should generate a log with the **404** status. You probably saw a log like this on `ElastAlert`:

`INFO:elastalert:Queried rule Alerting 404 from 2020-06-30 18:54 UTC to 2020-06-30 18:57 UTC: 2 / 2 hits`

`INFO:elastalert:Ran Alerting 404 from 2020-06-30 18:54 UTC to 2020-06-30 18:57 UTC: 2 query hits (2 already seen), 0 matches, 0 alerts sent`

`INFO:elastalert:Background configuration change check run at 2020-06-30 18:57 UTC`

`INFO:elastalert:Background alerts thread 0 pending alerts sent at 2020-06-30 18:57 UTC`

It means that our alert is working and I should have received a notification on Slack:

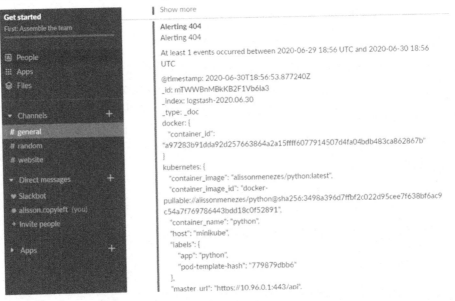

Figure 12.11

As you saw in the preceding image, I received the notification on Slack with the logs where I can see the error and check what is happening with the application.

Of course, you can explore more `ElastAlert` and configure different types of alerts, using email, for example. However, many companies now are changing from email to Slack or similar tools. That is why, I used it as an example.

Conclusion

This chapter was a short explanation of how we can set up an environment using the EFK stack and Kubernetes. The same steps work on Cloud or on-premises environments. This whole chapter aimed to show you a short explanation about everything that is possible to do using the DevOps technologies. For each chapter, we could have written a whole book. However, in my view, it is very important to have a general overview about different topics, because, you will be able to think what is possible to do and what the people are using for different cases. And after that, you can go deep in each one of the solutions represented here or find their alternatives.

Index

Made in the USA
Coppell, TX
02 August 2022

80788284R00142